CHRISTIAN FAMILY MATTERS

Christian Family Matters

Edited by

Ian Shaw

EVANGELICAL PRESS OF WALES

Cover photograph by Michael Rock

The choice of version for Bible quotations was left to the individual contributors. Unless otherwise indicated, Elwyn Davies, Douglas Jones and Neil Richards have followed the Authorized Version, and Ian Shaw, David Kingdon and David Potter the New International Version, while Brian Harris employs both. The initials NASB signify the New American Standard Bible, and RAV the Revised Authorized Version.

Earlier versions of Chapter 8 and the first section of Chapter 9 have previously been published in booklet form by the Evangelical Movement of Wales under the titles *Divorce* and *Abortion*.

Published by the Evangelical Press of Wales
Bryntirion, Bridgend, Mid Glamorgan, CF31 4DX
Printed by the Bridgend Printing Co. Ltd., Bridgend, Mid Glamorgan

Contents

About the Contributors

Sir Frederick Catherwood is Member of the European Parliament for Cambridge and North Bedfordshire.

J. Elwyn Davies is the General Secretary of the Evangelical Movement of Wales.

Douglas D. Jones, now retired, was for many years the Pastor of Trinity Baptist Church in Gloucester.

David P. Kingdon, until recently the Minister of Mount Zion Baptist Church in Cardigan, is on the editorial staff of the Inter-Varsity Press.

Stuart Olyott, formerly a minister in Liverpool, is Pastor of the French Baptist church in Lausanne, Switzerland, and author of several books.

David C. Potter is the Director of Christian Concern for the Mentally Handicapped ('Cause for Concern'), based at Reading.

Brian Harris is a Consultant Psychiatrist, working in Cardiff.

Neil C. Richards is the Minister of Wheelock Heath Baptist Church in Cheshire.

Ian Shaw is Lecturer in Social Work at University College, Cardiff.

Foreword

God has ordained three institutions for the good order of society, the family, the state and the church. Of these three, the family is the most basic, the one which continues when the others are in chaos. Down the centuries and in all kinds of societies, the family has held its place and society has retained some kind of cohesion—until now.

Today, in large parts of America, the divorce rate is up to 50 per cent and, even in more stable Britain, it is nearing a third. Grandparents and the wider family have provided some stability, but now grandparents are divorced and the wider family is dissolving too. Children are thrown adrift, juvenile crimes of violence against the person are soaring. As one chief constable said, 'If parents cannot control two kids, how can one policeman control two thousand?' Abortions of unborn children run into millions, matching even the holocaust. And the whole process of dis-integration is urged on by a rapidly expanding industry in commercialized sex.

The church itself is not immune. Pastors are now dealing with break-up of marriage in the church, and there are noticeable numbers of divorces between pastors and their wives. If the church is to stand out against this trend—and it must—then it has to see exactly where and why the trend is wrong. This book aims to do just that. It is based on God's revelation to mankind of the way in which He has made us and the rules which He has given us for our relations with each other. Today's trends deliberately confuse the relationships and discount the rules. The result is a most unhappy society. We not only have to protect ourselves from the chaos, we have the light to show the way to our neighbours. This book puts the light where it can shine.

FRED CATHERWOOD

Introduction

TO be in the world but not of the world is, for the Christian, a statement both of irreversible fact and constant aspiration. 'They are not of the world any more than I am of the world', Christ affirmed; and yet 'they are still in the world' (John 17:14,11). The Christian has been born again, and no longer belongs to this world. Yet Christ prays for the sanctification of His disciples, and the Christian will long for and, by God's grace, experience the increasing claims of God on every part of his life in the world.

We must beware at this point. The Christian faith does not consist simply in the act of worship. The Roman Catholic Church falls into this error by its tradition of regarding separation from the world as the highest achievement of holiness, and by regarding marriage as a sacrament. The Christian, however, will regard daily life in home and employment as equally a part of that pure and faultless religion which God requires as are the worship and witness of the local church.

The fact that we are Christians does not mean that we will be right in all we think or do. Indeed, one of the remarkable results of becoming a Christian is that it almost always raises new problems which the believer has never had to confront hitherto. The gospel compels you to think, just because it has something to say about the whole of life. The Christian faith speaks to and governs all we do and think, believe and practise. For this reason we are to be contemporary Christians, ever seeking to apply God's unchanging, authoritative Word to the changing social world in which we are placed, so that we are truly those who are both in the world and yet not of the world.

ATTITUDE TO FAMILY LIFE

The Christian is nowhere faced with a more acute challenge to think and live to the honour of God than in the sphere of the family. The challenge comes from a number of directions. During the post-war period a significant shift of attitude towards the family has taken place. The loss of any strong Christian influence on ideas of marriage and the family has removed any clear reason for faithfulness within marriage. Marriage is viewed as a kind of contract, in which people are held together only by what each puts in to and gets out of the marriage. Faithfulness becomes conditional on the continued success of the marriage. The relaxation of the divorce laws and the provision of legalized abortion both reflect this fragmentation of the family. Voices have been raised in criticism of the family from the women's movement and from many academics. Referring to the 'nuclear' two-generation family of parents and children, the BBC Reith lecturer Edmund Leach echoed the views of a growing number when he said, 'Far from being the good society, the family, with its narrow privacy and tawdry secrets, is the source of all our discontents.'

Against such views, it is not only the Christian who laments the decline of the family. Indeed, some people clearly regard the family as the only hope for a stable and happy society. Marriage, from this point of view, replaces God. The Christian views this over-optimistic faith in the family with extreme caution. Alan Storkey has wisely remarked that 'a human love relationship cannot bear the full religious weight that a person's relationship with God should carry . . . All men and women are sinners, and the time must inevitably come when they cannot inspire love and adoration.'[1]

A corresponding polarization of attitudes exists in our society towards parenthood. Families tend to be either child-centred or parent-centred. Child-centred parents emphasize the child's wants, and fail to recognize the child's sinful nature. As with King David in his old age, they never interfere with their children's lives by asking, 'Why do you behave as you do?' (1 Kgs. 1:6). Conversely, a parent-centred family may manifest itself in child neglect, the pursuit of careers or even pride in children.

In the face of this social quicksand, Christians are called to defend and exemplify the biblical view of the family. We are to be neither naïvely unrealistic nor unthinkingly traditionalist. Christians are sometimes too optimistic about family life. An appreciation of the authority given to parents or husbands, for example, will not of itself guarantee that all will be well. On the other hand, believers should not succumb to the bleak pessimism that regards the family as being on the brink of destruction at the hands of communism, evolutionary theory, educationalists, humanism, socialism and the women's movement! It is imperative that we understand what God's Word says about marriage and the family, and that we rest on Scripture alone. Without this foundation we will be at sea in the face of attacks on the Christian view of the family, unable to distinguish the important from the secondary, uncertain of our own position, and 'blown here and there by every wind of teaching' (Eph. 4:14).

Clarity and godly consistency at this point will provide a foundation for other areas of our Christian life. For example, David Kingdon points out later in this book the way in which the child's experience of authority within the family acts as a preparation for later life beyond the immediate circle of the family.

The contributors to this book share the belief that God's authoritative Word is worthy of our closest attention and demands our obedience on whatever topic it speaks. Husband and wife, parent and child—these relationships form the basis of family life. Rev. Elwyn Davies, Pastor Douglas Jones and Rev. David Kingdon expound and apply the fundamental biblical teaching on these questions. Some evidence about recent trends shaping family life in this country is summarized below, and the later chapters in this book seek to identify a biblical response to these trends. Extensive changes have taken place in the availability of means to prevent the birth of children, and Dr Brian Harris discusses the implications for the Christian of developments in birth control, sterilization and abortion. The Abortion Act, together with changing attitudes to illegitimacy, has dramatically reduced the number of children placed for adoption. However, the overall scale of the tragedy of separated and unwanted children has not diminished. In his discussion of fostering and adoption, Rev. Stuart Olyott brings both personal experience and application of Scripture to bear on this problem. Other children spend part or all of their lives suffering from handicapping disability of various kinds. Rev. David Potter points out the challenge to Christian churches and families posed by problems of this nature. Hitherto Christians have scarcely written anything about fostering, adoption, or physical and mental handicap.

Problems affecting children are often part and parcel of problems involving the parents. Rev. Neil Richards gives careful attention to the biblical teaching about divorce, and considers some of the pastoral issues that may arise.

One of the most fundamental developments in the Western world during the twentieth century has been the greatly increasing proportion of older people. The remaining chapter in this book considers the particular questions facing the older believer, and suggests ways in which the Christian church may fulfil her responsibilities in this area.

The writers of this book have tried to provide a way in to these questions, in the knowledge that 'there is much land to be possessed' if our hearts, minds and lives are to be biblically

11

renewed. Hence, each chapter concludes with suggestions for further study, selected from readily available sources, and offered as helpful starting-points rather than comprehensive guides.

Applying God's unchanging Word to a changing society is, therefore, our Christian responsibility. If we are to do this, we must be aware of the shape and character of the society in which God has placed us. This is not to say that the believer's task begins entirely anew with each generation. There is much to learn from the witness of Christians in previous generations. However, we cannot simply adopt the solutions of yesterday for the problems of today, without at least working out afresh the form of application. The developments which influence the family are in some cases distinctive features of the twentieth century.

Government figures help to indicate some fairly clear trends in the post-war period. We need to be cautious in interpreting the figures, and sensitive to the beliefs and attitudes which are sometimes assumed in such statistics. However, the broad canvas is clear. There has been a major breakdown of family values. This is not to say that things have never been worse, nor that we are on an inexorable downward slide. The Christian doctrines of providence and common grace, as we will see in the opening chapter, reveal the extent to which unbelieving families may demonstrate real mutual love, even beyond that experienced in some Christian families. That there is a problem, however, is clear to all but those most blinded by prejudice and preconception.

RECENT FAMILY TRENDS [2]

The figures for marriage and divorce reveal a marked rise in the number of divorces. The number of divorces per year has increased fivefold since 1961, and now stands at 150,000. Despite the fact that marriages are breaking down after a shorter period of time, children are involved in about six out of ten divorces. The Divorce Reform Act was passed in 1971, and the steepest rise in the number of divorces took place in the years immediately following. However, it would be misguided to see the legislative change as the *cause* of marriage breakdown. The divorce rate was already rising fast, and legislative changes are at least partly the effect of earlier changes of values. The total number of divorced people in England and Wales now stands at over one and a half million, compared with less than half a million in 1971.

Many people will have divorced and remarried; figures for these people are not included in this number, and neither are the many thousands of separated couples. Over a fifth of all men and women who marry are already divorced. In 1982, in a third of all marriages, one or other partner had been previously married. Add to this the knowledge that almost one in eight of women between the ages of 18 and 49 are known to be living with someone to whom they are not married, and the large-scale disappearance of the biblical marriage pattern becomes clear. Monogamy has partly given way to serial polygamy.

We should not exclude the significance of social factors from our understanding of this problem. When the church ceases to act as salt to the world in which it is placed, the resultant corruption will be shaped by the characteristics of the society of the time. In a helpful discussion of the current influence of socially depriving conditions on marriage, Bob Holman, a Christian community worker, points out the way in which working-class young people are pushed into early marriage, often against their better judgment, by their own family conditions. Once married, pressures on marriage are increased by financial problems, the effect of long-term unemployment and severe illness or handicap. For example, there may be over 400,000 families in Great Britain where the head of the family is unemployed. As Christians we need to be aware of such factors. 'Love, courtship, marriage, separation, divorce does not occur in a social vacuum'.[3] If we are to be truly an inconcealable city set upon a hill, our Christian witness and application of God's Word must be thoroughly worked out in the light of such evidence of the prevailing effects of the Fall.

Single-parent households have gradually increased in number over the last decade, and now stand at one and a half million. It is estimated that about 10 per cent of all children live in single-parent families.

Changing family patterns affect young children in various ways. For example, the rate of illegitimate births has risen sharply over the last 20 years, and now stands at over 16 per cent of all live births. This statistic is all the more remarkable when the abortion figures are taken into consideration. Were it not for the abortion legislation, it is probable that a far greater rise in the numbers of illegitimate children would have taken place.

The Abortion Act was passed in 1967. In 1969 a total of 50,000 legal abortions were carried out on women resident in England and Wales. In 1983 the figure stood at 127,000 (a figure which has remained steady since 1980). Over half of these abortions are carried out on single women. Just as disturbingly, the period since the passing of the Act has seen a dramatic rise in the number of abortions carried out on women under the age of 20. In 1969 the figure for England and Wales was 9,000. By 1983 it had risen fourfold to 35,000. In this context, we need to observe the growing number of sterilization operations. Information is not very precise, although a recent informed estimate suggested that up to 100,000 women, plus a smaller number of men, are being sterilized each year.

Trends in one area are associated with reverse trends in other areas. Recent years have witnessed a marked fall in the number of children available for adoption. Since 1976, adoption orders have fallen from 17,500 to about 11,000, and are still falling. Much of this fall is due to the decline in illegitimate children adopted by people other than their parents. In 1968, 60 per cent of all adoptions fell into this category. By the early 1980s the figure had fallen to 35 per cent—just 3,500 children.

There appear to be two major reasons for this trend. First, the Abortion Act has had a drastic effect on the number of illegitimate, unwanted children who would otherwise have been born. (Although, as we have seen, the actual number of illegitimate births is still rising, the abortion legislation has served to hide the far greater rise in the number of conceptions outside marriage.) Second, single parents have shown an increased willingness to keep their children, whereas previously they may have parted or been persuaded to part with them for adoption. One interesting development is the increase in the number of *legitimate* children adopted by people other than their parents. This perhaps shows a greater (and welcome) readiness on the part of people to adopt children with special needs, though we cannot be sure.

It is difficult to estimate the total number of children living away from their parents. Well-informed sources suggest that in the mid-1970s about 120,000 children were living away from their families, and the figure is unlikely to have fallen since that time. About 42,000 of those children would have been in foster homes, although the actual number of children entering a foster home in any one year will be much higher, because many such placements are for short periods.

Estimates of the number of handicapped children are extremely vague. We know that about 30,000 children under the age of 16 are registered as handicapped. However, such registration is voluntary, so these figures are certainly an underestimate.

We conclude this brief picture of family trends with information about the elderly in our population. Before the First World War the elderly of retirement age comprised less than 7 per cent of the population. Now the figure is 15 per cent. During the same period, the proportion of elderly people to numbers in the population of working age has risen from about 1:10 to 3:10. Between now and the end of the century the numbers of very elderly people will continue to rise. Women have a greater life expectancy than men. For example, three-quarters of those over the age of 85 are women.

All this has an important bearing on the family life of old people. More than a third of all elderly people live alone. However, whereas 20 per cent of elderly men live alone, the figure for elderly women is 45 per cent. There are now three million households in the United Kingdom which consist of a person of retirement age living alone— more than one in seven of all households.

May God grant us the grace to be truly biblical contemporary Christians, faithful to the day in which He has placed us.

IAN SHAW

NOTES

1 A. Storkey, *A Christian Social Perspective* (Inter-Varsity Press, 1979), p.202.

2 The figures in this section are taken from two current government sources, viz. *Annual Abstract of Statistics, 1985* and *Social Trends, 1985*. In most cases the latest figures available refer to 1983. A helpful series of publications is available from the Study Commission on the Family, 3 Park Road, London NW1 6XN. Of particular interest are *Happy Families?* (1980), *Values and the Changing Family* (1982) and *Families in the Future* (1983). While Christians will not agree with every interpretation and recommendation, these short books provide a valuable source of information and comment.

3 R. Holman, *Poverty: Explanations of Social Deprivation* (Martin Robertson, 1978), p.11.

1

The Bible and the Family

IAN SHAW

WHEN the Bible speaks about the family, it does so in the context of the great doctrines of creation, sin, faith, redemption, love and providence. We limit God's directives on family life to a set of moral rules at our own peril.

In the limited space available we can only sketch the broad outlines. First, our understanding of the biblical teaching must be founded on a realization of God's unfolding revelation within His Word. Second, families are patterned upon God's work as Creator and Preserver, marred by man's sinful nature, and, for the Christian at least, renewed by Christ's work as our Redeemer.

THE FAMILY IN THE BIBLE

The Bible uses several words for the family, and this should alert us to the fact that God's Word does not give a single, standard answer to the question 'What is a family?' The family in the Old Testament could refer to the father's house, the extended family or even the nation as a whole (1 Sam. 9:20f.; Gen. 7:1,13; Amos 3:2). There is no biblical word for the nuclear family, although the fifth commandment shows that it was recognized as a central part of the household. Family life took precedence over individual life, as shown by the way in which people regarded themselves as 'of the tribe of so-and-so'. Arranged marriages were typical, and a very high value was placed on marriage. To be unmarried was virtually to have no identity. Lineage mattered greatly; hence the extent of Abraham's sacrifice in leaving his country, his people and his father's household. The exodus from Egypt was organized in families. A lamb was to be sacrificed for each family, and instruction and recollection was to be centred in the family (Exod. 12:3,26; 13:14).

We can summarize the New Testament position by saying that Christ in part brought in a new situation, and in part renewed the original creation pattern. Thus, in Matthew 19, the Mosaic

17

concession on divorce is withdrawn and the original pattern is renewed.[1] Yet, furthermore, some would now make themselves eunuchs for the kingdom of God's sake—an unthinkable position for our Lord's contemporaries. Spiritual relations set kinship relations in a new light, as witnessed by Christ's gentle rebuke to His mother at the wedding in Cana (John 2:4).

However, the family is still central in the New Testament. Five times Christ exhorts His hearers to honour their father and mother. On two of these occasions His exhortation includes a condemnation of those who put religious offerings ahead of family obligations (Matt. 15:4-9; Mark 7:9-12). So although Christ's advent created potential for conflict in families, He lived in a family and blessed families, and this pattern, alongside the recurring call for instruction within families, continues throughout the New Testament (Acts 5:42; 10; 16:13-15,31-34; 18:8; 20:20; 1 Cor. 16:15; 1 Tim. 3:4,12; 2 Tim. 1:5; 3:14f.; Titus 1:5f.).

Christians should beware of dogmatism in asserting the precise biblical form of the family. David Kingdon warns us to avoid confusing matters of taste with the authority of clear biblical principle. An understanding of biblical teaching and history is of help to Christians who find themselves in widely differing cultures. In many tribal cultures family patterns are conditioned by religious traditions. Arranged marriages will trouble believers converted from an Islamic background. However, it may help to realize that the Bible does not condemn arranged marriages as such. Indeed, arranged marriages existed in the early church, and the Puritans, with their strong covenant theology, regarded such marriages with far more equanimity than ourselves. The modern ideal of romantic love scarcely exhausts biblical teaching. The abiding, permanent family pattern for the believer in the dispensation of grace derives from an appreciation of the implications of God's work as Creator, man's fall into sin and Christ's redeeming work.

CREATOR AND KEEPER

God made man in His own image. Indeed, it was male and female together that constituted 'Man' (Gen. 5:1-2). Neither men nor women can live autonomously, despite the more extreme arguments of some feminists, and neither sex is in any way superior to the other. However, a clear authority structure is established, thus indicating that submission does not equal inferiority. In so far as Christians have inferred this, they are in error, and so are those critics who impute such attitudes to Scripture.

It is possible that the early chapters of Genesis take us further than simply seeing each individual as made in God's likeness. The references to man and woman together as being in God's image (Gen. 1:27; 5:2) may suggest that it is in marriage and the family that the most complete expression of man as the image of God is found. Perhaps this is what Paul means when he speaks of 'the Father, from whom every family in heaven and on earth derives its name' (Eph. 3:14,15 NASB). Human dignity is founded upon this truth. David Potter points out just one application of it in showing that Scripture demands the full acceptance of those who are handicapped.

THE FAMILY AND THE FALL

We have already seen that some patterns of family life ignore the fact of human sinfulness. If we exalt marriage to a pedestal, or if we make our families child-centred, we are ignoring the effects of the Fall at our peril.

God's curse upon Eve was that He would greatly increase her pains in childbearing. 'With pain you will give birth to children. Your desire will be for your husband, and he will rule over you' (Gen. 3:16). There are two aspects to this judgment. First, as Elwyn Davies points out, it reiterates and underlines the relationship between husband and wife that God established before the Fall. In that sense, God's judgments are not arbitrary, but themselves contain the seeds of mercy. The Hebrew also suggests an increase in conception. Secondly, however, it contained a strengthening of the original law, thus increasing the woman's subordination. Calvin aptly remarks that Eve 'had, indeed, previously been subject to her husband, but that was a liberal, gentle subjection; now, however, she is cast into servitude'. The pull of sin is always towards instinctive 'desire' and dominating 'rule'. The corresponding judgment is made upon Adam, where fruitful labour becomes 'painful toil'. God is here making statements about what will be the case, and not commands about what ought to be the case.

Can I make what some readers may regard as a controversial inference? I am not too happy with a complete dismissal of the position taken by the women's movement. There are, of course, serious criticisms of feminist positions, because often they assume an inevitable incompatibility of interest between husband and wife. None the less, I think there is a point to be made about some men's oppression of their wives, which is simply a reflection of the awful result of the Fall.

How, then, will the knowledge of human sinfulness affect our understanding of families? First, it will save us from a romantic idealism in our expectations of family life. For example, in talking

19

about the position of the elderly, we shall see the dangers that may attach to a nostalgic picture of life. Similarly, our view of family life as a whole will be shaped by an appreciation of God's preserving providence in our sin-stained family relationships. It is unbiblical to regard the Christian home as a near perfect place. Sinners live there—but the sinless Saviour lives there too, and that is what makes the difference between a Christian home and the families of unbelievers. Secondly, an awareness of human sinfulness will preserve us from regarding men and women as no longer accountable for their actions. The Old Testament prophets were often called upon to deliver God's judgment upon the heathen nations surrounding Israel (e.g. Ezek. 25,32; Amos 1,2; Hab. 2). On what grounds did God hold these nations accountable? They were not in covenant with Him, and were the recipients of no divine revelation. Yet, as men with the requirements of the law written on their hearts, these nations—along with the unbelieving, spiritually ignorant people of our own society—were accountable to God for how they lived in their families and in society. To treat people as accountable is to offer real hope. Thirdly, because of God's preserving mercy, sinful men and women are not entirely abandoned to sin. Indeed, non-Christian families may in any given instance come nearer to biblical norms than a Christian family. 'Which of you, if his son asks for bread, will give him a stone? Or if he asks for a fish, will give him a snake? If you, then, though you are evil, know how to give good gifts to your children, how much more will your Father in heaven give good gifts to those who ask him!' (Matt. 7:9-11). We should remain ever thankful to God that 'evil' men and women are capable of loving family relationships.

THE FAMILY AND THE GOSPEL

Ask a Jew, a Hindu, a Buddhist, a Muslim, a Roman Catholic or many nominal members of Protestant churches, why they belong to their particular faith, and they are likely to reply, 'Because I was born or brought up as such-and-such.' Yet Christianity, rightly understood, is different from virtually all other religions. A Christian is not born but made.

A Christian is in covenant with God, and, as Elwyn Davies points out, that covenant is itself of the nature of a marriage bond. Thus, in the Old Testament, the Lord is spoken of as the husband of Israel, and the marital relation is seen as illustrating and reflecting the relation of God and His people. Hence, when Israel turns to other gods, she is an adulteress (Ezek. 16:23ff.). The same truth is taught in the New Testament, when Paul reminds the

Corinthians that their bodies are members of Christ. 'Shall I then take the members of Christ and unite them with a prostitute?' (1 Cor. 6:15). Peter makes a similar point, in reminding husbands that their relationship with their wives will affect their relationship to God. If we are inconsiderate, then our prayers will be hindered (1 Pet. 3:7).

If we are in covenant with Christ, 'There is neither Jew nor Greek, slave nor free, male nor female, for you are all one in Christ Jesus' (Gal. 3:28). This verse is often misapplied in order to set aside all distinctions between the sexes. Rather, Paul is here dealing specifically with the question of who may become a son of God, and on what basis. His answer is that the gospel is for *all* people who come to God on the basis of faith in Christ. He is not thinking about relations within the body of Christ, but the basis of membership.

We have seen already that Christ repeatedly exhorted His hearers to honour their parents, and condemned those who used religious responsibilities as a way of escaping from family obligations. Yet whereas for the Old Testament Jew faith and family lineage were so often inseparable, for the believer discipleship at once enriched, yet superseded, family allegiance.

Christ 'did not come to bring peace, but a sword'; quoting Micah, He characterized the coming of the gospel as setting 'a man against his father, a daughter against her mother, a daughter-in-law against her mother-in-law—a man's enemies will be the members of his own household' (Matt. 10:34-36; Mic. 7:6). There would even come a time when 'Brother will betray brother to death, and a father his child. Children will rebel against their parents and have them put to death' (Mark 13:12). By comparison with our love for Christ it may appear that we hate our nearest and dearest relatives, and even our own lives (Luke 14:26; cf. Luke 9:59-62). Christ Himself, when told that His mother and brothers were looking for Him, looked at those seated listening to Him and said, 'Here are my mother and my brothers! Whoever does God's will is my brother and sister and mother' (Mark 3:31-35).

We cannot leave this consideration of the way in which the gospel brought renewing blessing to the family without observing, as Elwyn Davies discusses in the next chapter, that the gospel shows a model of true marriage love. The mutual love of the husband and wife is not to be based on romantic love, feelings of love, adoration, obsession or love at first sight, but 'faithful, for better or worse, sacrificial love of the kind that Christ has for His church'.[2]

We noted earlier that Christ's teaching on the family was partly new and partly a renewal of the original creation pattern. The renewal of the creation pattern is clear in Christ's rejection, in Matthew 19, of the rabbinical debate about the grounds of divorce, and the demonstration that Moses' concession was brought in only because of God's hard-hearted, rebellious people. Again, it is the creation pattern that lies behind part of Paul's argument about the marriage relationship in Ephesians 5.

Singleness

What is striking and remarkable, however, is that Christ has something new to add, which has memorable application to the unmarried believer.[3] His removal of the Mosaic concession leads His disciples to conclude that celibacy may be an easier course than marriage. Only those to whom it is given can accept this teaching, Christ replies. The disciples were correct in assuming that some would remain single, but wrong as to the motive. 'Eunuch' was a stigmatizing term in Judaism, and Christ deliberately adopts it to speak of those who would remain unmarried for the sake of the kingdom of heaven. Our Lord 'was himself the prime example of a eunuch for the sake of the Kingdom'.[4]

Jeremiah is another person in Scripture who was denied the companionship of wife and family for the sake of the kingdom (Jer. 16:1-4). The apostle Paul firmly rejected the error of some Corinthians by insisting that those who married had not sinned. Yet he personally favoured the single estate, not because of obligation, but because it allowed him free devotion to the Lord (1 Cor. 7:29-35). Although he wished that all men were like him, he taught that 'each man has his own gift from God; one has this gift, another has that' (1 Cor. 7:7). Some are gifted to celibacy, some are not, and this is obviously related in part to age (1 Tim. 5:11-14). Thus, completely in harmony with Christ's teaching, Paul shows us that his singleness was for the purpose of devotion to the kingdom, not as a means of avoiding sin.

We may conclude from this that devotion to Christ in our own lives may be expressed either in faithful marriage or in the single state. There were women who ministered to our Lord's needs, and those who contended at Paul's side in the cause of the gospel, and it seems more than likely that a number of these would have been single women. In later centuries, how many faithful believers have sacrificed the prospects of marriage and family life, not because they were not eligible, but in answer to God's call to take the gospel to others! Henry Martyn was not the only missionary to have felt this sacrifice keenly, and yet be enabled to praise God for His grace in making up the loss to his soul.

22

Singleness for the sake of the kingdom looks forward to the full realization of God's purposes at the resurrection, when there will be neither marrying nor giving in marriage, and when the creation pattern will fade (Matt. 22:30). Until that time the single believer can claim the full blessing of the Messianic promise:

> And let not any eunuch complain, 'I am only a dry tree.' For this is what the Lord says: 'To the eunuchs who keep my Sabbaths, who choose what pleases me and hold fast to my covenant—to them I will give within my temple and its walls a memorial and a name better than sons and daughters; I will give them an everlasting name that will not be cut off.'
>
> Isaiah 56:3-5

An unbelieving partner

Liberal Christians are fond of saying that the twentieth century is so different from the first century that the gulf is fundamentally unbridgeable. Yet one problem evidently shared is that of Christians married to unbelieving partners. Christians must marry only in the Lord (1 Cor. 7:39); yet with the coming of the gospel the church was increasingly faced with situations where one of two married unbelievers had become a Christian.

This problem was nowhere more acute than in the church at Corinth, and God's Word has much to say to help both pastors and Christians facing the same problem at first hand today (1 Cor. 7:12-16; 1 Pet. 3:1-7).

Speaking authoritatively, as an inspired apostle,[5] Paul says that if the unbelieving partner wishes to continue the marriage, the believing partner has no right to take any initiative which would lead to the break-up of their relationship (1 Cor. 7:12,13). Why? Basically because they are 'one flesh', but this is not the whole reason. The reason given by Paul, which was most pertinent to the situation, is that the unbelieving partner and the children benefit from the continued marriage. The marriage partner is 'sanctified' by the believing wife or husband (v.14). This verse is difficult to understand, yet we can certainly say that the unbeliever is placed in a position of close proximity to the saving grace of God and thereby given an access to the gospel which would not exist if the believer was not in their midst. The power of the gospel is clearly illustrated: grace is more potent than nature. Through living with one who is praying for their salvation, and who is able to instruct in the gospel and demonstrate in daily living what Jesus Christ has done for them, the unbeliever 'tastes' the work of the Holy Spirit (Heb. 6:4ff.).[6]

How are unbelieving partners to be won for Christ? Speaking to believing wives, Peter emphasizes that husbands must see Christianity in their lives, and not simply hear about it: 'that they may be won over without talk by the behaviour of their wives' (1 Pet. 3:1). However, their behaviour is to be not simply a device to win an unbelieving husband, but something which is right in itself—'the unfading beauty of a gentle and quiet spirit, which is of great worth in God's sight' (v.4). The believer's motivation should be to please God. Marriage is never to be adopted as a method of evangelism.

Christian husbands are exhorted to live with their unbelieving wives 'in an understanding way' (v.7 NASB). The idea that women cannot be understood is unbiblical. The husband is to show that giving, considerate, understanding love which is exemplified in the example of Christ. His love will reflect the fact that his wife is 'a weaker vessel' (v.7), a fragile container, as Jay Adams gently expresses it. We are not to think that women are less reliable in moral judgment, or less intelligent. Peter may mean that the wife is physically weaker than the husband, or he may be conveying that she is in a weak position in relation to the exercise of authority. The New Testament teaching about the wife's submission does not mean that the wife is inferior in any way to the husband. Paul declares, 'I want you to realize that the head of every man is Christ, and the head of the woman is man, and the head of Christ is God' (1 Cor. 11:3). Clearly the woman is not inferior to the man, any more than Christ is inferior to the Father. There is division of labour and responsibility in the Trinity, and an analogous order, structure and division of responsibility within the home.

We indicated in the Introduction the spiralling number of single-parent families. David Kingdon rightly points out that the expression 'single-parent family' can be misleading if it points away from the realization that a family is not complete without both wife and husband. They need each other in order to be complete. However, as with unequal marriages, the existence of single parents represents a real challenge for our churches, and one which we have failed to meet. We must be alert to the difficulties of the children, and, assuming it is the father who is absent, the church must be ready to offer fathering. The challenge is particularly to the Christian men of the church, who need to be awake to the opportunities to spend time in a consistent, sacrificial way with fatherless children. It is but one manifestation of the Christian's duty to befriend other people's children, to which Stuart Olyott refers.

Family and Local Church

The coming of the gospel raised new questions for the relationship of God's people in their families and in the corporate gatherings for worship and witness. Scripture suggests four guidelines for our benefit and blessing. First, as we have already seen, God's requirements have primacy over the family, without countenancing the use of religious activities as an escape route from family obligations. We cannot but bemoan the frequency with which domestic responsibilities are wrongly used as arguments for neglecting the work of the church. 'I have just bought a field, and I must go and see it . . . I have just bought five yoke of oxen, and I'm on my way to try them out . . . I have just got married, so I can't come' (Luke 14:18-20).

Scripture also shows the separateness of church and home. The family is not a local church, and the local church is not our family. Home is the place to satisfy our hunger, not the Lord's table, is Paul's admonition to the Corinthians. The distinction between home and church is again brought out in the reminder from Scripture that home is a place of rest and withdrawal, particularly in times of discouragement. From the hour of Christ's death, John took Mary into his own home.

The third scriptural principle is that home is a place of testimony and preparation for gospel work. How eager was the man from Gadara, delivered from the evil spirit, to follow the Lord Jesus! But Christ is unequivocal in His response: 'Go home to your family and tell them how much the Lord has done for you' (Mark 5:19). The only witness to the truth that the ten cities of Decapolis had was through the faithfulness of this one man. Behaviour at home is preparation for the work of the church in two respects. First, it provides a grounding for mature members (1 Tim. 5:4; Titus 2:5). Secondly, it is an indispensable qualification of those who would hold office in the church, for if anyone does not know how to manage his own family, how can he take care of God's family, the church (1 Tim. 3:4,5,12)?[7]

Finally, the New Testament has much to say about hospitality. We are both to show hospitality and to receive it. While Christian families have obvious opportunities in this sphere, it is quite clear that the requirement to be 'given to hospitality' extends to every church member. We are to 'offer hospitality to one another without grumbling' (1 Pet. 4:9), and if this is expected of every Christian according to his ability and opportunity, it is all the more a requirement of those who hold office (1 Tim. 3:2). It is important to add that when we have entertained our friends and relatives, we have still not begun to exercise hospitality in the full New

Testament sense. Those who are less well off, least able to give recompense, newcomers, or sufferers for the gospel, are the people referred to in Scripture, and not just the well-known visiting preacher.

It is less widely appreciated that Scripture has rich guidance for the recipients as well as the suppliers of hospitality. A particular privilege of church membership is the access it gives to the homes of fellow members. We are to receive this hospitality in the right spirit. It gave David pain to recall that 'Even my close friend, whom I trusted, he who shared my bread, has lifted up his heel against me' (Ps. 41:9). Without exception, we are to respect the hospitality we receive. Christ instructed the 70 disciples (Luke 10:1-11) to remain with the first family that offered them hospitality, implying that they were not to move around in search of the best hospitality, but graciously accept it in the spirit in which it was given. Also, they were to 'salute' each house as they entered it. Applied to ourselves, it must mean at least that we go out of our way to further the well-being of that family, and remember them in our prayers, as Paul did Onesiphorus (2 Tim. 1:16-18). In conclusion,

> Be not shy; do not suspect your welcome, nor be afraid of being troublesome, but eat and drink heartily such things as they give; for, whatever kindness they show you, it is but a small return for the kindness you do them in bringing the glad tidings of peace.
>
> Matthew Henry

May we work both to give and receive hospitality in this spirit.

NOTES

1 The so-called exceptive clause, 'except for marital unfaithfulness' (Matt. 19:9; cf. Matt. 5:32), is discussed by Neil Richards in a later chapter.

2 A. Storkey, *A Christian Social Perspective* (Inter-Varsity Press, 1979), p.210. J. E. Adams, *Update on Christian Counselling II* (Presbyterian & Reformed, 1981), pp.34-48, gives a practical exposition and application of 1 Corinthians 13, which is worth reading in this connection.

3 I am heavily indebted at this point to James Hurley's superb exposition in *Man and Woman in Biblical Perspective* (Inter-Varsity Press, 1981).

4 Hurley, *Man and Woman in Biblical Perspective*, p.106.

5 Paul's careful distinction between his own words and those of the Lord—'I say this (I, not the Lord) . . .' (1 Cor. 7:12)—has sometimes troubled Christians. Is the apostle making a distinction between the inspired and authoritative statements

of Christ, and his own uninspired judgments? This interpretation ignores the fact that Paul speaks 'as one who by the Lord's mercy is trustworthy' (v.25, cf. v.17). Paul's intention is to show that he is applying Christ's teaching to a new area, while making it plain that Christ did not speak directly to the issue. Christ spoke only of marriage relations between believers, and not of marriages where one partner is an unbeliever.

6 If the unbelieving partner chooses to leave, the situation is rather different (vv.15,16). The importance of these verses for the biblical teaching on divorce is considered carefully by Neil Richards in Chapter 8. See also John Murray, *Divorce* (Presbyterian & Reformed, 1961), pp.62-78.

7 Great emphasis has been placed on this in Gary North's important article on 'Family Authority and Protestant Sacerdotalism' (*Journal of Christian Reconstruction*, 4, 1977-78, pp.87-129). He has much to say that is thoughtful and valuable, in his comments on preparation for the ministry, the priesthood of all believers, the convolutions in the reformed doctrine of eldership, the significance of the child, and the importance of the family as the training ground for the faithful. However, his article is dangerously marred by a number of untenable conclusions, which stem from his particular application of Meredith Kline's covenant theology, and his associated failure to distinguish adequately between the old and the new covenants. He advocates the active participation of the children of believers in the Lord's supper, the requirement of marriage as a qualification for church office, the baptism of households, including unconverted wives, and a marked separation of baptism and church membership (North, 1977, pp.87-129). David Kingdon discusses some possible implications of covenant theology in his chapter on childhood.

FURTHER READING

Many Christian books have been written on the family. Jay Adams' work provides a useful starter, particularly his *Christian Living in the Home* (Baker, 1972), and his series of five tapes on *The Christian Family* (available in this country from Alethean Publications Trust, 17-19 Watergate Street, Whitchurch, Salop, SY13 1DP). Larry Christenson's *The Christian Family* (Bethany Fellowship, 1970) has been reprinted many times. Of particular interest are 20 tapes by Geoffrey Thomas on *Biblical Perspectives on the Family* (obtainable from Christian Reformed Tapes, 72 High Street, Inverurie, Aberdeenshire). The best available published sermons are those by Dr D. M. Lloyd-Jones in *Life in the Spirit* (Banner of Truth, 1974), pp.83-302.

James Hurley, *Man and Woman in Biblical Perspective* (Inter-Varsity Press, 1981), chapters 4 to 6, is most valuable for placing our general understanding of the family in its biblical framework. Hurley should also be consulted for his thorough discussion of the biblical teaching on the role of women, although this covers a number of important questions not directly relevant to this book.

Susan Foh, *Women and the Word of God* (Presbyterian & Reformed, 1979), has also made a helpful contribution on this topic, and S. Rees (ed.), *The Role of Women*, Part I (Inter-Varsity Press, 1984), may also be recommended. Finally, Banner of Truth Trust (3 Murrayfield Road, Edinburgh, EH12 6EL) have made available four excellent cassettes by A. N. Martin, on *Distinctive Sexual Identity*.

2

The Marriage Covenant

J. ELWYN DAVIES

The husband and wife relationship has been subjected to such abuse in our day that we are compelled to ask how long the concept of marriage, as traditionally understood, can continue as an accepted feature of the society to which we belong. When we take into consideration the high incidence of broken homes, the 'latchkey children' phenomenon, the proliferation of single-parent families, and the singularly unfulfilling marital relationships which seem to be on the increase everywhere, what is left of family life in Britain today falls far short, to say the least, of what God ordained for mankind. At times it is barely recognizable.

The statistics, as we know, are ruthlessly candid. Twelve years ago one in ten marriages ended in divorce. Today the ratio is one in three, children being involved in three out of four such marriages.[1] In the USA the ratio is already one in two. According to the latest Government report,[2] one in every six children born in Britain is illegitimate.

The tragic consequences are all too evident. Among divorcees, admissions to psychiatric hospitals are reported to be eight to ten times higher than among married couples, and the mortality rate two to three times higher. Meanwhile, as happened in Harringay not so long ago, militant feminists merrily smash shop windows, damaging wedding dresses as a protest against marriage! Nowhere do we see more starkly the tragic legacy of this wanton and often deliberate debasement of what God ordained for the good of mankind than in the lives of a sullen and rebellious generation of young people who have never known the security of a stable and caring parental relationship.

A broken home, an emotionally deprived child, a battered wife, even overburdened social services, only serve to remind the Christian of what is so sadly evident in every other aspect of man's existence—the heart-rending consequences of his attempt to throw off completely the shackles of God's law and government. The

Christian will not be unduly shaken, but he will be distressed. For he, more than anyone else, realizes how different life on earth would have been if man had not rebelled against God in the first instance. He may well reflect on two things. First, nothing short of a mighty outpouring of God's Holy Spirit, leading to a thoroughgoing abhorrence of the self-centred and indulgent practices of our day, can stem the tide of decadence and infidelity which now threatens to engulf our society. Secondly, only the overall supremacy of God's sovereign sway could have obliged nations and peoples throughout history to conform as closely as they have done —and will yet be required to do—to the pattern God ordained in creation:

> And the Lord God said, It is not good that the man should be alone; I will make him an help meet for him . . . And Adam said, This is now bone of my bones, and flesh of my flesh: she shall be called Woman, because she was taken out of Man. Therefore shall a man leave his father and his mother, and shall cleave unto his wife: and they shall be one flesh.
>
> Genesis 2:18,23-24

In the light of this knowledge of what the Creator Himself has ordained for mankind, Christians are confronted with a twofold obligation. First, if they are married, they are clearly called upon to honour to the full the kind of relationship which God has intended for husband and wife. Secondly, whether married or not, they are to commend that prescription in all its fulness to those who enter into that relationship, doing so as those who believe that all God's laws reflect His glory and are therefore beyond reproach. They must not fall into the pitfall of commending it in isolation, since it forms only a part (albeit an integral part) of God's prescriptive will for mankind; nor must they commend it simply on the ground that it is superior to every other prescription for married life. Along with every other commandment and precept, God's ordinance of marriage and His prescription for those privileged to enter that estate are not options to be preferred; they are mandatory. The God who made us has no intention of renouncing His proprietary rights. What was ordained in creation, and subsequently reinforced most emphatically by the Lord Jesus Christ during His earthly ministry (Matt. 19:3-12), applies to all marriages, not simply the marriages of Christians. It is only as men and women acknowledge God's precepts, as they apply not only to the marriage relationship but also to the whole of life, that they will begin to appreciate the wisdom of His ways and the amazing beneficence that lies behind them.

THE DIVINE PRESCRIPTION

When we turn to consider God's commandments with respect to the 'holy ordinance of matrimony', we find first that it is His will that those who become husband and wife should continue in that estate until they are parted by death, the only permissible ground for divorce being adultery. We also find (and this is our present concern) that God the Creator has exercised His divine prerogative in making known to men and women the ways in which they are to be related to each other within marriage. Finally, upon examining His words we discover that different attitudes, and therefore very different disciplines, are called for from each partner. For these reasons, all who contemplate marriage, or who hope that this may one day be their privilege, ought to examine with the utmost care what God says will be required of them as husband and wife respectively, and what, in turn, they have the right to expect from their partner. They may have been brought up in a home which enjoyed a tolerably happy parental relationship, or even in a Christian home where the parents avowed allegiance to the Word of God, but they ought not on this account to assume that God's precepts for marriage were honoured to the extent that they should have been. Furthermore, since so much joy and satisfaction, both for themselves and also for others, hinge upon their achieving within marriage the kind of relationship which God has ordained, they simply cannot afford to go wrong through lack of forethought.

Indeed, sociologists today are insisting that if marriages are to survive contemporary pressures, priority has to be given *throughout married life* to what they call 'improving the quality of the relationship'. Those of us who maintain that we are in possession of the Creator's own instructions must not fall into the error of thinking that a brief, cursory glance, just prior to taking our marriage vows and only occasionally thereafter, will suffice. Nor must we think that because we are Christians these things will resolve themselves. Nothing could be further from the truth. Placed as we are under the awesome and yet glorious obligation of working out our own salvation with fear and trembling (Phil. 2:12), we cannot take for granted a relationship which affects so profoundly not only our own joy and performance in life, but also that of our partners and, even more seriously, of the children whom God in His wisdom has entrusted to our care. So we turn to the teachings of the Word of God.

We see in the creation narrative the measure of the priority and absoluteness which God has ascribed to the marriage relationship. As with so many truths stated in embryo in the Old Testament, this was to be given fuller elaboration and clarity in the New, first by

31

the Lord Jesus Christ Himself, and then through the writings of the apostles. Of all such writings, none is more helpful than the apostle Paul's remarkably full treatment of the subject in Ephesians 5:22-33. We shall base our present study upon these verses, bearing in mind other scriptures, and particularly those which speak of God's purposes in creation.

Wives, submit! husbands, love!

The first intimation of the distinctive roles which God had purposed for husband and wife was given in the words already quoted, spoken by God when He created man and woman (Gen. 2:18). Their significance was underscored in the way in which they were created:

> And the Lord God formed man of the dust of the ground, and breathed into his nostrils the breath of life; and man became a living soul . . . And the Lord God caused a deep sleep to fall upon Adam . . . and he took one of his ribs, and closed up the flesh instead thereof; and the rib, which the Lord God had taken from man, made he a woman, and brought her unto the man.

> Genesis 2:7,21-22

It is significant to note that, *whenever* the husband/wife relationship is under discussion in Scripture, the injunction is always the same:

a) The wife is always instructed to *submit* to her own husband (Eph. 5:22,24,33; Col. 3:18; Titus 2:5; 1 Pet. 3:1,5,6; 1 Cor. 11:3), and

b) the husband is invariably commanded to *love* his wife (Eph. 5:25,28,33; Col. 3:19; 1 Pet. 3:7).

Except in the more restricted context of Paul's exhortation in 1 Corinthians 7:3, where he has particularly in mind the more intimate side of married life, these are the terms in which it is always presented. Never once do we read, 'Husbands, submit! wives, love!' In Titus 2:4-5, where the apostle is explaining in some detail the duties and obligations of young women in particular, he does preface the injunction to obedience with the need also to love their husbands, but this exception in no way invalidates what is clearly an apostolic emphasis.

How then are we to understand this stubborn insistence on 'Husbands, love! wives, submit!'? The fact that women are not commanded to love their husbands cannot possibly mean that they are to submit to them *without* loving them! The Scriptures clearly take the view that if a woman is prepared to submit herself to her husband throughout her life, she must be motivated by the highest considerations of love and concern for his well-being. The apostle's insistence can mean only one thing. *With respect to what God has intended for married life, where the wife will fail is when she usurps the place of her husband and insists on having the final say. Where the husband will fail, and sin equally grievously against God, is when, insisting on his rightful place in the home, he ceases to be a loving and caring husband.*

There is surely nothing more grievous in Christian circles than to hear a husband constantly holding forth that he is the 'head of the home' and that his wife must always submit to his judgment, when at the same time he shows little or no awareness that the Scriptures insist with equal firmness that he is to love his wife to a degree which surpasses all other examples of human love and affection. And if the husband is afflicted with an inordinate sense of his own importance, he can find all manner of subtle ways of justifying taking his wife and her labours completely for granted. On the other hand, there are more ways of establishing a matriarchal regime in a home than for a wife to stamp her feet or brandish her fists! Dark retaliatory moods, awesome brooding silences, biting words of sarcasm, constant bickering and nagging, overt references to shortcomings (delivered preferably in the presence of others)— these form part of the devastating list of all-too-familiar behavioural patterns in a wife's armoury of resistance and eventual subjugation of her husband. Both attitudes are equally wrong and sinful.

This is where we have to begin. Married couples are under orders. Whether they like it or not—even if at times they doubt whether the other partner is deserving of such an attitude—wives are to submit to their own husbands in everything, and husbands are to rule and to love. To an age which has arrogantly set aside those religious convictions which have influenced our culture so beneficially in the past, such scriptural injunctions may be totally abhorrent. Nevertheless this *is* God's prescription, and He never enjoins anything upon His creatures without having very good reasons indeed.

WIVES, SUBMIT!—BUT WHY?

When we turn to the passage in Ephesians we find that, although the apostle offers a very detailed explanation as to why husbands should love their wives, he seems to make no attempt to explain why wives should submit to their husbands 'in every thing'—none, that is, except for the phrase 'as unto the Lord' (v.22), and the rather blunt assertion, 'For the husband is the head of the wife' (v.23). The phrase 'as unto the Lord' indicates that this submission on the

33

part of the wife is what the Lord requires of her; the husband is head of the wife by divine appointment. Just as, in Ephesians 6:5, servants are commanded to obey their masters with fear and trembling and in singleness of heart as an act of obedience to the Lord ('as unto Christ'), in like manner, and for the same reason, must wives behave towards their husbands (though no one would suggest that the relationship is the same). Similar sentiments are expressed by the apostle Peter. In 1 Peter 3:1 he commands wives to be in subjection to their own husbands, requiring this on the same basis as all the other commands in the preceding chapter (2:13-25). The only reason given is 'for the Lord's sake' (2:13).

So, on the surface at least, it seems from these passages that wives are required to accept this injunction without explanation and without question. Elsewhere in the Scriptures, however, we find that a more than adequate explanation is given, and this leads us to conclude that the reason why the apostle did not expand on it to the Ephesian Christians was because they already knew. Some of them would have been Jews, and therefore conversant with Old Testament teaching; others would have been converted to the Christian faith for some time, and so would be well-versed in Christian truth. In addition—and this would apply to Jew and Gentile alike—Paul knew that they would have an innate awareness of this by virtue of that body of truth intrinsic to all human beings—the law of God 'written in their hearts, their conscience also bearing witness' (Rom. 2:15).

Such a statement calls for explanation. When God made man, He made him 'in his own image'. In other words, in certain important respects man was to resemble God; because he bore a likeness to certain of the attributes of God, there would be a measure of affinity. Though at first sight the words 'Let us make man in our image, after our likeness' seem to refer to man alone, it is evident from what follows that the woman was also to share in these characteristics: 'let *them* have dominion . . . male and female created he them' (Gen. 1:26,27). So we rightly deduce that both man and woman were created in God's image. Having created them, God said to them both: 'Be fruitful, and multiply, and replenish the earth, and subdue it: and have dominion over the fish of the sea, and over the fowl of the air, and over every living thing that moveth upon the earth' (Gen. 1:28).

However, while at *this* point in the narrative no distinction of roles is suggested with respect to rule and government, when we turn to the separate and distinctive account of the creation of man and woman in Genesis 2 the story is very different. In the first place, we find that priority was given to man in the order of creation (Gen. 2:7,8). Secondly, before woman was ever created, man was given the primary role in government and leadership. It was the man whom the Lord God put in the garden of Eden 'to dress it and to keep it' (v.15). It was to the man that He gave the prohibition, 'of the tree of the knowledge of good and evil, thou shalt not eat' (v.17). And it was to the man that He brought 'every beast of the field, and every fowl of the air . . . to see what he would call them: and whatsoever Adam called every living creature, that was the name thereof' (v.19). Thirdly, and most convincingly, it was because the Lord God knew that it was not good for the man to be alone that He determined to provide 'an help meet for him'[3] —one who would be able to assist him in ways that would best of all correspond to his needs and responsibilities. Such a helper could not be found among the beasts and birds, and so God made the woman especially for the man (vv.21-22).

It is evident, then, that the woman was made by God not simply as an idle companion to relieve man's boredom and loneliness, but rather as the best and most appropriate help the Almighty Himself could devise for man *as he faced the duties and responsibilities laid to his charge*. Thus assisted, he would be able to fulfil the awesome role of leadership and government decreed for him. The woman's role, therefore, was to be a pivotal one.

The subordination of her life to serve man's calling and obligations to Almighty God was further reinforced after the Fall. Indeed it was a major component in the penalty God meted out to the woman and her posterity as a consequence of her sin: 'Unto the woman he said, I will greatly multiply thy sorrow and thy conception . . . thy desire shall be to thy husband, *and he shall rule over thee'* (Gen. 3:16). This last element in the punishment was not an act of thoughtless revenge. It was imposed to reinforce what God had intended in creation. The God who had made her 'of the man . . . for the man' (1 Cor. 11:8,9) knew that in some respects the woman would be more vulnerable than the man. She would be 'the weaker vessel' (1 Pet. 3:7); 'the woman being deceived was in the transgression' (1 Tim. 2:14). So, notwithstanding the possibility that man would often prove himself utterly unworthy of the submission and service his wife would give him, the woman was sentenced to that subjection. In other words, the curse strengthened and made more inevitable what God had already purposed.

What God was doing at this point is analogous to what He had to do later with mankind generally. Instead of obeying His command to fill the earth and subdue it, which would obviously have entailed dispersal and migration, they decided to build a city and a tower, and make a name for themselves, 'lest we be scattered abroad upon the face of the whole earth' (Gen. 11:4). But God intervened and by confusing their tongues forced them to comply with His sovereign will: 'So the Lord scattered them abroad from thence upon the face of all the earth' (v.8). Diversification of language, although undoubtedly a punishment, was also a blessing in disguise, for it served to compel men to do what God had all along intended. In exactly the same way, the curse upon the woman obliged her to do what otherwise, through sin, she would not have been at all inclined to do.

Reflecting God's glory

This is why the Scriptures insist that although both man and woman were made in God's image, it is only man who partakes of the 'glory' that belongs to God. An essential aspect of God's glory is that He should rule in the affairs of heaven and earth. That glory is His by right. Remarkably, He has chosen to give something of that glory, in a limited context, to man. Although made in the image of God, woman does not partake of this glory. This is the point which the apostle Paul argues so strongly in his letter to the Corinthians:

> But I would have you know, that the head of every man is Christ; and the head of the woman is the man; and the head of Christ is God . . . For a man . . . is the image and glory of God: but the woman is the glory of the man. For the man is not of the woman; but the woman of the man. Neither was the man created for the woman; but the woman for the man.
>
> 1 Corinthians 11:3,7-9

In the light of this biblical explanation it is not surprising to find the Scriptures reminding us that this difference which characterizes the woman will have a limiting effect upon her service and usefulness in situations other than the home:

> Let the woman learn in silence with all subjection. But I suffer not a woman to teach, nor to usurp authority over the man, but to be in silence. For Adam was first formed, then Eve. And Adam was not deceived, but the woman being deceived was in the transgression. Notwithstanding she shall be saved in childbearing, if they continue in faith and charity and holiness with sobriety.
>
> 1 Timothy 2:11-15

Indeed, it is this same lack or disability, disqualifying her from having the rule in the home, which the apostle Peter had in mind when he urged husbands to give 'honour unto the wife, as unto the weaker vessel' (1 Pet. 3:7). A husband gifted by God with the

36

capacity to rule—an endowment which clearly implies the ability to think rationally and dispassionately—could so easily become impatient with his wife, who would be more inclined to follow her feelings and instincts. Hence the apostle Paul says, 'Husbands, love your wives, and *be not bitter against them*' (Col. 3:19).

So the Scriptures *do* explain why wives are to subject themselves to their own husbands. To say that this is proof of anti-feminist bias in the apostle Paul is utter nonsense. The responsibility for the injunction rests not with the apostle but with God. That is why Paul does not hesitate to say that women 'are commanded to be under obedience, *as also saith the law*' (1 Cor. 14:34), and 'Wives, submit yourselves unto your own husbands, *as it is fit in the Lord*' (Col. 3:18). That is also why the apostle Peter urges wives married to unbelieving husbands to submit to their authority in the home. In his judgment, this attitude, backed by a morally upright and God-fearing life, could help to win the unbelieving partner to the faith; so convinced is he that the husband's natural instincts will tell him that this is right and proper in a woman:

> Likewise, you wives, be submissive to your own husbands, that even if some do not obey the word, they, without a word, may be won by the conduct of their wives, when they observe your chaste conduct accompanied by fear.
>
> 1 Peter 3:1-2 RAV

Similarly Paul, commenting on the spiritual potential of a right attitude in believing partners, whether husband or wife, writes:

> For the unbelieving husband is sanctified by the wife, and the unbelieving wife is sanctified by the husband: else were your children unclean; but now are they holy.
>
> 1 Corinthians 7:14

The only reason

Before we turn to consider the husband's obligations towards his wife, there is one further question we have to ask. What is the significance of Paul's reference to Christ as 'the head of the church' and 'the saviour of the body' in the context of a wife's attitude towards her husband (Eph. 5:22-24)? It has been suggested that this introduces an additional reason why *Christian* wives (for it could apply to no one else) are to submit themselves to their husbands. We affirm without hesitation that this is to mis-understand what the apostle is saying here; what is worse, it serves to weaken the force of the scriptural teaching on the obligation of every wife, whether Christian or not, to submit to her husband.

37

The apostle's reference at this point to the headship of Christ over His church is intended not as a further reason, but rather as a helpful example or illustration. The words of verse 23, which come between two exhortations to submission, take the form of a firm assertion: 'For the husband is the head of the wife, *even as Christ is the head of the church: and he is the saviour of the body.*' Far from introducing something new, the apostle is undergirding and confirming what he has already said in the phrase 'as unto the Lord'. The *one* reason why wives are to be submissive to their husbands is because it is God's will and decree that they should be so. Just as it is God's will and appointment that His Son should be the Head of the church and the Saviour of the body, so it is God's will and appointment that every husband, whether Christian or not, should be the head of the wife and, as we shall see later, the saviour of the body. The only difference between the Christian and non-Christian wife in this respect is that the former, who has yielded her life to the Lord and who loves the Saviour, is able to profit from the illustration.

And that, we hasten to add, is no mean consideration. The position of headship given to the Lord Jesus Christ over His people constitutes a glorious reminder to the Christian wife of the position of rule and responsibility which God has appointed for her husband. In the same way, the obligation of the church to submit to her Lord serves for the Christian wife as a gracious but compelling reminder of her obligation to submit to her husband. The enlightenment she has received on becoming a Christian enables her to profit from the analogy. It also increases her responsibility to honour God's prescription. In no way, however, does it lessen the obligation of every wife, Christian or not, to obey what God has ordained in creation.

To the Christian wife who is married to a Christian husband, the illustration of Christ as Head and Saviour of the church also conveys the truth that her husband is to love her as Christ loved the church. The analogy holds good equally for both partners! For the Christian husband there could surely be no more compelling illustration than this. What could bring home to him more powerfully his obligation to love, care for and protect his wife than the example of the Lord Jesus Christ and His saving love for the church?

It is to the husband's responsibility that we now turn. And we must do so with care, for in studying the relationship between married couples in the light of the remarkable teaching given to Christians in Ephesians 5, we must be careful to relate the *essential* element in what the apostle is saying to *all* mankind. That is why we shall have to begin again with God's creation ordinances.

38

SAVIOUR OF THE BODY

The God who made woman *from* the man, *for* the man, did not intend man, thus privileged, to treat God's gracious gift and provision as a chattel or slave. It is His will that a man should respond with protective love, and with a profound sense of gratitude for his wife's tremendous contribution to their life together. That is why God chose to take a part of man, and from it to form a woman. It is also why, as our Lord assures us, when two people are married, it is God Himself who joins them together so that they become one flesh—not in any metaphorical sense, but literally or '*meta*-physically' (Matt. 19:4-6). This is God's chosen way of creating between two people an attachment in the realm of the flesh which is unique, and which is intended to inculcate a sense of pride and possession in man akin to that which he feels towards his own flesh. Men and women do not have to be Christians for this to happen. For *any* husband, therefore, to treat such a privilege lightly constitutes the worst kind of ingratitude, and a grievous insult to the Creator. For a *Christian* husband to do so betrays the worst conceivable form of conceit; for, apart from the gift of eternal life—which is itself in the nature of a marriage bond, the Lord Jesus Christ and the sinner being made one in the realm of the spirit (1 Cor. 6:17)—in the realm of personal relationships there is no greater gift that he can receive.

So we hasten to do what the Scriptures always do—place alongside the duties and responsibilities of the wife those of the husband. The passage in Ephesians states them clearly and unambiguously, fully embracing all that is enjoined upon the husband elsewhere in Scripture. Indeed, these verses go further than any of the other scriptures, for they include this most helpful analogy of the Lord Jesus Christ's relationship to His church.

As in the verses addressed to wives, this section begins with a command followed by an illustration:

> Husbands, love your wives, even as Christ also loved the church, and gave himself for it; that he might sanctify and cleanse it with the washing of water by the word, that he might present it to himself a glorious church, not having spot, or wrinkle, or any such thing; but that it should be holy and without blemish.
>
> verses 25-27

Unlike the verses addressed to wives, however, the apostle follows this up by arguing that it is the most reasonable thing in the world to expect a man (whether Christian or not) to love his wife in this

39

way, *because of what God brings about when two people come together in wedlock:*

> So ought men to love their wives as their own bodies. He that loveth his wife loveth himself. For no man ever yet hated his own flesh; but nourisheth and cherisheth it . . . For this cause shall a man leave his father and mother, and shall be joined unto his wife, and they two shall be one flesh.

> verses 28,29,31 (quoting Gen. 2:24)

This is why it is reasonable to expect *every* husband to love his wife: they have become one flesh. Here the apostle, writing to Christians, draws an analogy between a man's attitude towards his own flesh (that is, his wife) and the Lord Jesus Christ's attitude towards His own people. Just as husbands and wives have become one flesh through wedlock, so Christians have become part of Christ's body, the church: 'For we are members of his body, of his flesh, and of his bones' (v.30). And just as men love their bodies, so Christ loves His church. The analogy is perfect. Not only has Christ loved His church as His bride, but He also loves her as His body; she is both bride and body to Him. The apostle introduces this not merely to illustrate how a husband should love his bride, but to show that what happens between the Lord Jesus Christ and members of His church is analogous to what happens between a husband and wife. In the former case, His people become 'members of his body, of his flesh, and of his bones': in the latter, they become 'one flesh'.

This, then, is the measure of the Creator's desire that a husband should love his wife. He has so made us that considerations of gratitude and indebtedness should compel us to love our wives. Further, we cannot but do so, for they have become part of ourselves. A woman taken from man has through marriage become one flesh with man again!

Again we say that the fact that the apostle is writing these things to Christians does not mean that what he has to say has no application to others. While it is clearly an advantage to the Christian to have this sublime example of how a husband should love his wife, it does not make the responsibility of the non-Christian husband to love his wife any the less, for the union between non-Christians is no less real than that between Christians. It does mean, however, that the Christian's responsibility is all the greater. The example of this twofold parallel of the Lord Jesus Christ as both the loving Head and the Saviour of His body ought to move him with the desire to please God in fulfilling what He has ordained for marriage—the more so in that he and his wife are willing subjects of that Head and privileged members of that body. In other words, while it would be true to say that a Christian husband, having the advantage of this illustration, ought to be a better husband, we cannot concede for a moment that it lessens the responsibility of all husbands to love their wives, this being an essential part of what God has ordained for mankind.

A husband's obligations

We would do well, therefore, by reference to this analogy, to ponder carefully the obligations that devolve upon the husband.

First of all, the husband is to *rule*. He must never evade or shirk his responsibilities as the head of the home. All major decisions concerning the home and the family are ultimately his responsibility. This does not mean, of course, that he will never confer with his wife or seek her counsel. Indeed, if as a Christian he looked to the Lord to lead him to his wife—that same Lord who, in creation, made the woman so that she could offer the most appropriate help to man—it will come as no surprise to him to find that she is admirably suited to his needs. What a tragedy it is when Christian wives have reason to despair of their husbands because they fall short of the requirement that they should rule! As a result they have often been left with no alternative but to settle for a reversal of roles, to the inestimable loss and chagrin of all concerned.

Secondly, the husband is to rule *as Christ rules as Head of the church*. In other words, he is so to rule as to inculcate in his wife a spirit of trust and confidence that will make it her delight and privilege to submit to him and support him in everything. He is so to rule as to give his wife every encouragement to fulfil her own potential also, not only in her God-given role as his 'helpmeet', but also in her God-ordained role as the child and servant of the Lord. The marriage relationship, after all, forms only a part of God's prescriptive will for mankind. The husband must not allow a sinful preoccupation with his own selfish interests to hinder his wife from daily placing herself at the disposal of her Lord, as she endeavours to serve Him first in her role as wife and mother, and then in every other aspect of their lives together. The portrait in the book of Proverbs of the caring and initiative-taking woman is a challenge to all husbands who would wish to make exorbitant and restrictive demands upon their wives (31:10-31). The heart of many a Christian husband has delighted in the knowledge that he too can 'safely trust in' such a wife (v.11).

Thirdly, the husband is to rule *in love*. He who is to rule his wife as Christ rules His church must love his wife as Christ loves His church. Indeed, it is only because the husband is to rule and care for his wife *as* Christ rules and cares for His church that wives are required to submit themselves to their husbands: 'For the husband is the head of the wife, even as Christ is the head of the church: and he is the saviour of the body. *Therefore* [on that understanding only] as the church is subject unto Christ, so let the wives be to their own husbands in every thing' (Eph. 5:23-24). In a spirit of sacrificial love the husband is to have an eye constantly to his wife's spiritual well-being and blessedness. With true devotion he is to care for her eternal interests as well as her temporal needs, jealously seeking that by her virtue and godliness she may become yet more worthy of his pride and esteem. Verse 25 reminds us of Christ's love for His church in the past —'even as Christ also loved the church and gave himself for it'. Then in verses 26-29 we are reminded of His love in the present—'that he might sanctify and cleanse it with the washing of water by the word, that he might present it to himself a glorious church, not having spot, or wrinkle, or any such thing; but that it should be holy and without blemish . . . the Lord [nourisheth and cherisheth] the church.' No sacrifice was too great to make—not even the death on the cross—so that He could eventually present His spouse to Himself. To the same end, no present need will go unmet, but He will nourish and cherish her daily. It is in this way that husbands are to love their wives.

Fourthly, the husband is to rule in love, *constantly reminding himself that he is actually nourishing and cherishing his own flesh!* As we have seen, in setting before his readers the example of Christ's love for His church and describing Him as Saviour of the body, the apostle is insisting that the bond or union effected between two persons in marriage is similar to that which obtains between Christ and His church. In both relationships the otherwise separate and distinct parties have become one body.

In other words, apart from the consideration that husbands are under orders to love their wives as Christ loved the church, God has so constituted us physically that this becomes not a burdensome imposition but the most natural thing in the world! It would be against nature, and against all the instincts God has implanted in us, says the apostle, for husbands *not* to love their wives. By agreeing to become his 'helpmeet' for life, the wife has become the husband's 'other half' or, as some chivalrously insist, his 'better half'. This is so not in any metaphorical sense, nor as a flight of poetic fancy, but in actual fact. Between two people thus joined together a bond is forged in the realm of the flesh which can only be 'put asunder' by the forging of a similar union with another partner. 'What God hath joined together' nothing else will sever. It is God's obvious design and intention to compel the man—or, better, to make it eminently reasonable to him—to cherish his wife as he cherishes his own body.

Therefore, just as it is natural for a man to strive hard and long to care for his own body, so *for exactly the same reason* it is to be expected that those who are married will strive with equal care and tenacity to provide for the needs of their wives. It is God's way of ensuring that the one who has to a large extent forfeited her right to herself, surrendered her body and all her talents, subordinated all her plans and ambitions to those of her husband, and agreed for the remainder of her days to seek to help him in every way that she can, should not be allowed to suffer, *even though, by God's own decree, her husband has the rule over her*. It has been pithily expressed by Matthew Henry:

> The woman was made of a rib out of the side of Adam; not made out of his head to top him, not out of his feet to be trampled upon by him, but out of his side to be equal with him, under his arm to be protected, and near his heart to be beloved.

In submitting herself to a man who dwells with her according to *this* knowledge (1 Pet. 3:7), a woman has nothing to fear. Fear would be as inappropriate to her as it would be for Christians to fear the One who loved the church and gave Himself for it.

HEIRS TOGETHER

Since it is God's prescription for wives to submit and husbands to love, we can go on to affirm without fear of contradiction that marital bliss depends on the degree to which husbands and wives conform to this divine pattern.

Nothing makes a man happier than to be assured that the one who has graciously consented to be an heir with him of the grace of life (1 Pet. 3:7) confidently expects him to be able to cope with his responsibilities. Apart from the grace of God which is its source, nothing in life is more calculated to make him the man he desires to be for God and others. By the same token, nothing in life is more likely to undermine a husband's confidence and sap his energy and sense of well-being than to have to contend constantly with a partner who in one way or another will always insist on having the final say.

Similarly, nothing will give to a woman a greater sense of contentment and well-being than the knowledge that she has invested her life to help one who is capable of shouldering the responsibilities God entrusts to his charge. Such a wife has the added comfort of knowing that God would not have asked this service of her, had He not at the same time written it into the contract that the husband should love her as Christ loved the church, and as he himself loves his own body. Just as the Lord Jesus Christ delighted to share with His disciples the things His Father had told Him, and for that reason refused to call them servants (John 15:15), so she would rightly expect that, with equal candour, her husband would confide in her, so that, having his best interests always at heart, she would be able to offer help and counsel. The only qualification would be that her husband, under God, would be allowed to rule—a responsibility which, with a measure of relief or even delight, she should gladly leave to his charge.

*   *   *

We conclude our study where we began. Those who are contemplating marriage, including those who are in the early stages of courtship, should give to these considerations the utmost priority. Is this the relationship into which God is calling them? Is this the way they can see themselves relating to one another for the rest of their lives? Likewise, those who are already married, even though they may have enjoyed many years of married life, ought constantly to examine their lives in the light of the precepts laid down in Scripture. If they have reason to fear that their relationship is not as it should be, they have three questions to ask: (1) Is the defect due to ignorance? Have they studied the subject as thoroughly as they should have done? (2) Could it be due to sin? (3) Might it be that, because of some imbalance in their own parental background, they have been seriously prejudiced against achieving the kind of relationship which is ordained and commanded by God?

It is no secret that there can be considerable unhappiness even in Christian homes. In many instances this is due not so much to ignorance or wilful sin, but to an inbred prejudice, a fear that to comply with the terms of the divinely prescribed relationship would result in something which husband or wife may have had reason to fear or resent in early childhood. A wife will often find it difficult, or wellnigh impossible, to shake off distrust of a man's authority in the home if she (or her mother) were made to suffer at the hands of a selfish, self-indulgent or cruel father. Conversely, a husband may have had to put up with a self-centred, overpowering mother, who manipulated husband and child at will to serve her own selfish ends. Instead of inculcating in the son a capacity for trusting his

44

wife and expressing spontaneous appreciation of her services, this experience will have made him full of suspicion and unease, always on guard lest his position in the home be threatened or his legitimate desires ignored.

For the relationship which God has ordained for husband and wife to be prejudiced from the start or even placed in jeopardy for such reasons, is extremely tragic. Understood in its true biblical balance and perspective, this relationship brings untold joy and satisfaction, not to one but to both partners, and that satisfaction is enhanced, not lessened, as the years go by. The more the husband cares for and protects his wife, expressing ready appreciation of her devotion both to himself and to the home and family, the more she is encouraged to be an even better helpmeet. The more the wife shows by her life that she delights to promote his interests and well-being, the greater his response of love and gratitude. And so it goes on—or is meant to go on—in an ascending spiral of contentment and joy and ever-deepening confidence in one another.

There is no other way to overcome difficulties and problems with respect to married life than by first of all acknowledging that these things we have been considering are not options. They are commands. Wives, submit: husbands, love! We cannot improve on God's prescription, nor must we try to do so. If things are not working out in our marriage as they should be, we should first of all search our own hearts before God, to see if there is any hindrance in our own lives which is preventing us from obeying Him. We should also listen most carefully to what our partners have to tell us concerning the relationship, seeking all the time to ascertain exactly where we may be failing each other and disobeying God. If a relationship is under strain, there can be no better advice than for both partners to make it a practice to repeat what each understands the other to be saying. (In matters which lie so close to the heart, and upon which we can be unduly sensitive, it is surprising what poor listeners we can be.) If this does not help, we should without delay seek the advice of a pastor or an elder—one who would be able to assess the situation and diagnose the point of failure, with a degree of impartiality of which we ourselves at the time may not be capable. Not to do so is to perpetuate untold sufferings for ourselves, and to forfeit unsurpassed joy in the most intimate areas of our life. If we imagine for a moment that we can immunize our children against injury, hurt and disappointment, we are of all men most deceived.

Finally, God's laws are always intended to further His gracious purposes, and the commands given to husband and wife are no

45

exception. God's intention is that the relationship should be such that our 'prayers be not hindered' (1 Pet. 3:7). The man who has learnt to be considerate of his wife will also be considerate towards others. The discipline of having to take into account his wife's needs as well as his own will make him sensitive to the needs of others, including particularly those of his children. Learning to acknowledge with gratitude his indebtedness to his wife will teach the husband to be more alert to the service others render him, and much more prepared to respond with appreciation. If he is a pastor, he will be considerate towards his members, and never guilty of merely lording it over his flock.

On the other hand, the man who has thoughts only for himself and takes his wife very much for granted will inevitably distance himself from his children and will make a very poor spiritual leader. This is why the requirement that an elder should rule well in his own house is much wider in its scope than 'having his children in subjection with all gravity' (1 Tim. 3:4). It also includes his relationship to his wife—a fact rarely mentioned by many who wax eloquent about the father's rule over his children. 'For if a man know not how to rule his own house, how shall he take care of the church of God?' (v.5).

Similarly, the wife who has refused to submit to her husband and who insists on her own opinions and judgments will make a poor mother. She will have forfeited the discipline that would have helped her to think of others, and to subordinate her own desires to the desires of those entrusted to her charge who depend upon her love—a discipline which is the best possible training for one privileged to be the bearer of children (1 Tim. 2:15).

NOTES

1 Some 150,000 divorces were granted in 1983, almost double the 1971 total, and the proportion of divorces within four years of marriage has increased from 13 per cent in 1971 to over 20 per cent in 1983—*Social Trends* (published annually for the Central Statistical Office by HMSO), 1985.

2 *Social Trends* (HMSO), January 1985.

3 When in everyday conversation we refer to a wife as a 'helpmeet', we are bringing together two words which need to be kept apart if the meaning is not to be obscured. The King James version of Genesis 2:18,20 reads 'a help meet for him', meaning a help or helper appropriate for man.

FURTHER READING

A number of helpful books have been written on the subject of marriage. Jay Adams, *Christian Living in the Home* (Baker, 1972) has much to say that is of value. Christian couples may find the workbook approach stimulating. If so, the most complete text available is Wayne Mack, *How to Develop Deep Unity in the Marriage Relationship* (Presbyterian & Reformed, 1977). Perhaps the finest account of marriage as a creation ordinance is found in John Murray, *Principles of Conduct* (Inter-Varsity Press, 1957). An exposition of the verses discussed in this chapter can be read in D. M. Lloyd-Jones, *Life in the Spirit* (Banner of Truth, 1974), pp.83-234.

3

Parenthood

DOUGLAS D. JONES

Parenthood is the God-given norm for the married state. Ours is a generation which has seen the breakdown of family life, with dire consequences for all areas of society. The centrality of parenthood needs reasserting at a time when the mutual satisfaction of marriage partners is increasingly regarded as an end in itself, and when a growing number of people have apparently made a conscious decision to remain childless. Scripture offers no support to this position, and if young Christian couples are being drawn by such views of parenthood they should beware.

There may be limited exceptions to this principle. If there would be serious risks to the mother's health, or clear genetic evidence of probable disability to the children, we should not be too ready to criticize Christian couples who decide to remain childless. However, the general principle holds good that children are a heritage of the Lord.[1]

There are times when God, in His infinite wisdom, sees fit to leave a couple childless. This will be a cause of deep sadness. In Chapter 6, Stuart Olyott encourages Christian couples to consider fostering and, where possible, adopting children. Furthermore, having seen in the opening chapter that singleness offers special opportunities to the believer, why should we not view childlessness in a similar way?

THE GIFT OF CHILDREN

There is nothing quite to be compared with the joy of holding your firstborn in your arms for the first time. Birth announcements in a local newspaper often include mention of 'God's gift' of a son or daughter. One wonders how many parents who have had these words inserted really appreciate their implications. Scripture is clear on the subject. 'Children are an heritage of the Lord' (Ps.

49

127:3). 'It is he that hath made us, and not we ourselves' (Ps. 100:3). 'He giveth to all life, and breath, and all things . . . in him we live, and move, and have our being' (Acts 17:25,28). Jacob described his children as those whom God had graciously given him (Gen. 33:5), and parents who have been brought by divine grace to saving faith in the Lord Jesus Christ will surely do likewise.

It is a great privilege to be entrusted with parenthood, but with it comes an equally great responsibility. Once a little one has arrived, your marriage and home will never be quite the same again. He or she is going to become part of your life, and in due time may well be joined by others. There are many parents who will tell you that the event has enriched their marriage to a degree they could never have imagined.

However, this is not so with all. Sometimes fathers and mothers are unwilling to make the sacrifices associated with the arrival of a baby in the home—which only goes to show how unprepared they have been for marriage itself. The mother who farms out her children from a few weeks old so that she as well as her husband can go off to work has never really understood motherhood. We should not assume that the wife is the only one to blame in such situations. It is frequently the husband who covets the extra money, or who fails to help his wife find satisfaction in her role as mother. Neither are we insensitive to the real occasions of necessity which may arise, as when the husband is chronically ill, or when long-term unemployment has driven the family into considerable financial difficulties.

There are other parents, however, who build their lives round their children so that they take first place in everything, to the exclusion of the due relationship that should exist between husband and wife. It has been pointed out that God did not put parent and child in Eden, but man and wife. I have known cases where a woman has so given herself to her children and caused her husband to take second place that it has resulted in their having very little in common. Through the years they have grown apart, and by the time the last child leaves home there is very little left of the marriage. Harm has been done not only to husband and wife but to the children also.

Who is this little one who comes into our lives? A pastor visiting a Christian couple who were rejoicing over their firstborn was asked provocatively by the young wife, 'Who do you think he is like?' Taking a good look at the child, the pastor replied, 'Very much like Adam.' He was bringing a timely reminder that every child born into this world is not only involved in Adam's guilt but inherits his nature, and this will soon become evident as the child develops. Every Christian parent should understand that the need of their child for regeneration is identical with that of any adult.

Many older parents did not have the opportunity of watching the early development of their children. For fathers serving in the Forces during the Second World War, precious indeed were the visits home on leave which enabled them to see their children's progress since they were last at home. On one such occasion my wife and I were standing on a railway platform and I was holding our little son. A gentleman who obviously felt he was addressing a proud father asked, 'What do you want him to be when he grows up?' I think my reply took him by surprise. 'A Christian', I said. The greatest longing my wife and I had for our children, before any ultimate academic success or social position, was that by the grace of God they might come to a saving knowledge of the Lord Jesus Christ. In fact, we started praying for each of them before they were born. It is with thankfulness to our heavenly Father that I am able to say that our prayers were answered. Each of them is now married to a Christian partner and God has blessed them with their own children, for whose salvation they in turn pray daily.

NURTURE AND ADMONITION

Concern for the spiritual and general well-being of our children involves more than our prayers, important as these are. The apostle Paul writes, 'And, ye fathers, provoke not your children to wrath: but bring them up in the nurture and admonition of the Lord' (Eph. 6:4). The fact that he addresses fathers does not mean that he is belittling the role of mothers, for he has already included both parents in the position of authority over their children: 'Children, obey your parents in the Lord: for this is right. Honour thy father and mother' (Eph. 6:1-2). What reason are children given for obeying their parents? Not because it is safe to do so; not because parents are bigger, stronger, 25 years older, or wiser; not out of fear or even from feelings of natural affection. Parents are to be obeyed because the Lord has so ordained it in His perfect wisdom, and therefore 'this is right'. If we rest on any of the subordinate reasons, admirable as some of them may be, we shall find that one day some or all of them will no longer hold true.

The child's obedience should be the outward evidence of respect and honour. Charles Hodge aptly remarks that the word 'has reference to the inward feeling as well as the outward conduct'. Al Martin tells a story which perfectly illustrates the point. A little boy in church with his parents is told repeatedly to sit down. Eventually his parents plant him firmly on the seat, at which their son has the last word—'I'm sitting on the outside, but I'm standing on the inside!'

In addressing his words to fathers Paul reminds us of the divinely instituted order of the headship of the man—a principle discussed fully by Elwyn Davies in the previous chapter (Eph. 5:22-33; 1 Cor. 11:3). It has pleased God to assign to the husband the task of being the head of the wife, and hence also of the family. There is something quite pathetic about a husband who has allowed this God-given order to be reversed, and it is a sad fact that this has happened in many Christian marriages, with serious repercussions in church life. It is the father who has the *ultimate* responsibility for the upbringing of the children.

The verb used for 'bring up' (Eph. 6:4) is translated as 'nourisheth' in Ephesians 5:29, where Paul speaks of a man nourishing his own flesh. Its use in the former text indicates an active and positive engagement in the task of bringing up children; it conveys the thought of rearing tenderly and looking after with devoted attention. For the Christian parent this entails more than feeding and clothing our children, and nursing them when they are sick. It means showing our love for them by spending time with them, sharing their joys and their sorrows, showing them that they really matter to us.

Many churches seem to have to rely for their helpers on a faithful nucleus who are engaged in more activities than they ought to be, while others are 'passengers'. It is just here that there is a danger of neglecting our families. Some of the worst behaved children are those whose parents are busiest in church work. This may well be due to resentment on the part of the children, caused by the fact that their parents do not give time to them. Ministers and their wives need to be specially aware of this danger. They should try to overcome it by making sure that the manse is also a home, and by maintaining an interest in those things which interest their children individually. In our own family experience, holidays are partic- ularly important and hold for us some of our most treasured memories.

The state system in Britain means that schooling for children is compulsory and free education is available for them. One effect of the growth of this system has been that parents have tended to have less and less control over the training of their sons and daughters. From an early age, children from Christian homes come under teaching which is the very antithesis of those truths and principles which are dear to their parents. Not only are they taught evolution as if it were established fact, but the study of comparative religion puts Christianity into the same category as all the others, and what is taught about the Christian religion is frequently not in terms of biblical revelation. By contrast, Christian parents are not simply to bring up their children in terms of general morality and good behaviour, important as these are, but they are to relate all to that which is 'of the Lord'. All must be of Him and related to Him.

Notice that Paul, in speaking of this training, makes mention of the two elements of 'nurture' and 'admonition'. The word translated 'nurture' was applied in classical Greek to the training and education of a child. In scriptural usage it also implies the necessity of correction or chastisement to effect thorough discipline. Although not exclusively so, the word stresses training by *act*, and a better rendering would perhaps be 'discipline'. The word 'admonition' means literally a 'putting in mind', its distinctive feature being training by word of mouth, by what we say in actual words. We might render it as 'instruction'. Thus, while 'nurture' or 'discipline' refers primarily to what is *done* to the child, 'admonition' or 'instruction' refers primarily to what is *said* to the child.[2]

THE ACT OF DISCIPLINE

Christian parents who understand the doctrine of original sin will realize that their children need devotion, but also discipline. We have lived through a time of violent reaction to the rigid Victorianism of earlier generations. Discipline is sadly lacking in many families, including Christian ones, although there are those who have been brought to realize the dangers of permissiveness advocated in the early writings of Benjamin Spock and others. At the end of the Second World War we heard endless talk from 'experts' in the educational field about the need for 'self-expression' in children. What a harvest we have reaped as a nation in following the counsel of people who have no understanding whatsoever of the total depravity of human nature! Not that this is a new problem. Eli's sons 'made themselves vile, and he restrained them not'; and of David's son Adonijah it was said, 'His father had not displeased him at any time in saying, Why hast thou done so?' (1 Sam. 3:13; 1 Kgs. 1:6).

In this matter of discipline, when I hear a man say, 'I've never had to raise a finger to any of my children', I am forced to one of three conclusions: he has a very bad memory; he is a stranger to the truth; or else the man is just plain stupid and has a prospective delinquent on his hands! One of the speakers in a BBC radio discussion said he could understand a speaker smacking a child in temper, but was appalled at what he described as 'a smack in cold blood'. It need hardly be said that this is almost the exact opposite of how a Christian should regard discipline. It is sinful to punish a child because we have lost our temper, and those of us who have ever done so have repented bitterly of it; but the Bible clearly teaches parental responsibility in relation to correction. We read in the book of Proverbs, for instance: 'He that spareth his rod hateth his son: but he that loveth him chasteneth him betimes'; 'Foolishness is bound in the heart of a child; but the rod of correction shall drive it far from him'; 'A child left to himself bringeth his mother to shame' (13:24; 22:15; 29:15). Far from being cruel, discipline by act, properly administered, reveals that true devotion is associated with it. I am sorry to say that there are a lot of woolly-minded Christian parents who reveal a great lack in this respect.

Nevertheless we should remember that Paul says, 'Provoke not your children to wrath' (Eph. 6:4). In the corresponding verse in the Colossian letter (3:21) the apostle adds 'lest they be discouraged'. Discipline is intended not for the gratification of the parent but for the good of the child. All need to guard against using authority with such rigour that there is no attendant kindness. Parents who are always bawling at their children may cause them to lose heart through perpetual fault-finding, so that they resign themselves to believing that it is impossible to please. Rather, we should take every opportunity of commending our children and encouraging them all we can.

If discipline is to be properly exercised, then parents must mean what they say. It is of great concern to find that many Christians are not consistent in word and act. A child is told to do something and quite deliberately does not do it. Father or mother says, 'If you don't do it, I shall smack you.' The child still does not obey, and instead of the promised smack there ensues a long argument between parent and child, which the latter usually wins. Similarly, a child may be told that if he does a certain thing again he will be sent to bed. Knowing full well that the threat will not be carried out, the child does it again and is *not* sent to bed. Parents who fail in this way are making a rod for their own backs, and they will feel its smart very keenly in years to come.

How vital, too, that father and mother are consistent with each other in the way they exercise discipline! There is the kind of mother who over-corrects the children during the day, and then when father comes home from work he lets them do practically what they please. Little wonder that the children look upon mum as a horrible tyrant and dad as what he is, a fool!

I am not suggesting that our efforts will produce children in whose mouths butter would not melt, and who will never give us an embarrassing moment (we have all had red faces at times!). But if we neglect discipline we will raise spoilt, ill-mannered children whose conduct will always show up our failure as parents.

THE TEENAGE YEARS

Parents sometimes say, 'I'll be so glad when the children are not little any longer, and they'll be off our hands a bit more.' However, problems of a different sort still exist. There is widespread juvenile delinquency in our modern society which constitutes a grave problem. The attitude of many adolescents towards their parents can be summed up in the proverb which says, 'There is a generation that curseth their father, and doth not bless their mother. There is a generation that are pure in their own eyes, and yet is not washed from their filthiness' (Prov. 30:11-12). The children of Christian homes have to be at school and later at work with those of their own age who show that kind of utter disrespect.

A Christian psychologist has said that the proper time to begin disarming the teenage time-bomb is 12 years before it arrives. He observed that perhaps the most difficult problems referred to him occur with the rebellious, hostile teenager for whom the parents have done everything wrong since he was born. When we loudly deplore the evils of our day we are apt to forget that moral deterioration is inevitable if it goes unchecked. If parents do not exercise proper discipline when their children are small, they are likely to find it extremely difficult to do so when they become teenagers.

How is discipline to be exercised by Christian parents with teenage children? With loving devotion and prayerful desire for their highest good. But if we go on treating them as if they were infants we shall be making a great mistake. There are emotional conflicts within them during this period; they find it hard to analyse what they feel, and adolescence can be a time of considerable uncertainty. There is the desire to be independent and grown-up, but coupled with this is a sense of insecurity. Often young people do not really know what they want. In such a condition they can fall under wrong influences in the company they keep and the places to which they go. Certain people in the world of entertainment, art and literature know full well how to exploit the tendencies of this stage in the life of the teenager, often with disastrous results.

If ever there were a time when young people should be able to share things with their parents it is at this time. The trouble is that

55

their feelings are so complex that father and mother are just about the last people to whom they can bring themselves to turn, because they do not want to feel they are dependent upon them any more. Parents need to exercise much patience over this period, for unless they understand these symptoms they will be badly hurt. Those who formerly experienced closeness to their children now find there is a certain distance between them. When they were small, sons and daughters had their choices made for them, but now they want to make their own decisions, and the less their tastes are like those of their parents, so much the better in their estimation! As for advice, it is difficult to tell them anything; they know it all, or so they believe! Consequently there are occasions when the daughter can make her mother feel extremely small, and the son does not even want to acknowledge his father when his friends are around. It would be well for parents to understand that this kind of independence is often far more superficial than may appear, and this stage will eventually pass. Within the atmosphere of a home in which father and mother are true believers in the Lord Jesus Christ, seeking to apply faithfully the principles of God's Word, their family can be helped through this perplexing period of their lives. What young people long for most of all is certainty and security, and such a home should give it to them.

THE WORD OF ADMONITION

Adolescence is the period when children will form their own conclusions as to whether or not the professed faith of their parents is genuine. They will see if it is working out in the home in husband/wife and father/mother relationships and in dealings with other people. They may well ask some very searching questions about the Christian faith, some of the things which they readily accepted when small now becoming matters of serious questioning with them. Even if by this time they have come to a saving knowledge of the Lord, they will still want an authoritative answer to things which perplex them. Christian parents need to ask themselves whether they are sufficiently established in the faith to be able to give it. Sadly, not all parents are so established. Of course, not every father ought to be a budding theologian, but there is a regrettable tendency for parents to delegate the responsibility for the spiritual nurture of their families to the church of which they are members, and particularly to the Sunday school and children's and young people's meetings. While we gladly recognize the value of these, the initial responsibility lies at home. It is fathers who are exhorted to bring up their children in the 'admonition [instruction] of the Lord' (Eph. 6:4). The same principle is set out in Deuteronomy, where the responsibility is seen not just as a national matter but as a family matter too. Moses tells the Israelites, 'And these words, which I command thee this day, shall be in thine heart: and thou shalt teach them diligently to thy children' (Deut. 6:6-7). The word used here for 'teach' is not the normal one; it includes the idea of making an impression as well as giving instruction. God's words were to be impressed diligently, indeed deeply, upon the children. Instruction was to be thoroughly and conscientiously carried out. The things which the Lord commanded were to be the subject of conversation as they sat at home, when on a journey, when they retired to rest, and when they rose in the morning. We are to surround our children with the influence of them, with the prayer that they will grow up to regard every part of life from God's viewpoint.

How much are the things of God part of the conversation in our homes, even on the Lord's day? There are homes where there is plenty of conversation about what is going on in the activities of the church, and even some where father and mother criticize other people at breakfast, dinner, tea and supper; but that is not instructing children in the things of God, and it may well be doing a lot of harm. Many a preacher can tell the people to whom his ministry is acceptable or otherwise by the attitude of their children towards him!

As we read the Old Testament we see that in the Jewish home it was obviously anticipated that children would ask questions. While they were required to respect their parents, they were not expected to be 'seen and not heard' as some of our Victorian forbears demanded. At the observance of the Passover the children would ask, 'What mean ye by this service?', and the head of the household would be expected to tell them, 'It is the sacrifice of the Lord's passover, who passed over the houses of the children of Israel in Egypt, when he smote the Egyptians, and delivered our houses' (Exod. 12:26-27). It was the same with the twelve stones taken from Jordan and set up as a memorial. When the children asked, 'What mean these stones?', they were to be told, 'Israel came over this Jordan on dry land. For the Lord your God dried up the waters of Jordan from before you, until ye were passed over . . . that all the people of the earth might know the hand of the Lord, that it is mighty: that ye might fear the Lord your God for ever' (Josh. 4:21-24).

David Kingdon makes an important distinction between formal and informal instruction. Perhaps we may describe it as a distinction between planned and occasional or opportunistic instruction. The benefits flowing from fruitful, planned teaching of the gospel to our children are truly incalculable. However, it may surprise us to discover that our children are not the only beneficiaries. Parents may often feel that they gain at least as much blessing from the exercise as do the children. Through reading with their children, parents will grow in their own spiritual appreciation of the gospel. For example, they are repeatedly obliged to explain their faith, and we are all familiar with the pitfalls which lie beneath the apparently simple questions asked by children! Such questions are God-given opportunities, and we should aim to be as clear and faithful as we possibly can in our answers. There are further benefits too. During those difficult patches in relationships between parents and children, the daily meeting around the Word of God preserves an invaluable means of keeping open the lines of communication.

What principles should shape the times of reading and prayer with our children? The following brief guidelines may be of help. Start early in the child's life; keep to a regular time; do not be too long or too short; vary your approach, using reliable story-Bibles, workbooks and biographies, but without neglecting the text of Scripture; be thorough; avoid the extremes of anxiously pressing for an act of faith, or omitting all reference to the need for personal faith and repentance; gradually encourage times of prayer and Scripture reading in the privacy of their own room. Remember that Christian homes are not the only ones that may benefit from parents reading good books with their children. Try putting Marian Schoolland's *Leading Little Ones to God* in the hands of those with young children, praying that God will make it a blessing to them.

The book of Judges warns us of the consequences if we neglect the word of admonition. 'And there arose another generation after them, which knew not the Lord, nor yet the works which he had done for Israel' (Judg. 2:10). Some of our forefathers were most faithful in showing the praises of the Lord to the generation to come, but there has arisen a generation which does not know these things. Just as there had been such a decline in Israel, so it is in the Christian church, and part of the blame for this lies with parents. Some Christians seem far more concerned about their children's secular education and careers than they are about their spiritual welfare. One is saddened to hear of homes where instruction is never given in the truths of God's Word, and the family seldom, if ever, read it together and pray together. On the other hand, where there is vital family worship, there is a spiritually healthy family. Children are to be brought up in the 'instruction of the Lord', and this is not something to be delegated to the Sunday school. (This, after all, was originally designed for the purpose of reaching children—and parents—from unbelieving families.)

I recall my visit several years ago to the home of a young Christian couple. The father had come in from a busy day at work, and the mother had been equally busy in the matters of the home. As soon as tea was over, they and the three children gathered at the table for a time of family devotions. The youngest was still not old enough to understand the words to be read or the prayers offered, but she was not left out. After the reading the two boys, aged seven and five, were asked questions by their father about what had been read, and they replied with enthusiasm. Following this they and their parents bowed their heads, and each prayed in turn. I know that home well. The upbringing of the children is attended by many of the usual problems attached to temperament and so on, but my heart rejoices that the practice continues daily with obvious profit as this father and mother seek to bring up their children in the discipline and instruction of the Lord.

Matthew Henry's words make a fitting conclusion:

> I know that you cannot give grace to your children. Nor is spiritual life the guaranteed outcome of a spiritual upbringing. But if you make it a matter of conscience to teach your family, if you teach them the good and right doctrines of the Bible, if you counsel them and warn them about false paths, reprove, exhort and encourage them, if you pray with them and set them a good example, then you will have done your part, and you may leave the rest to God.

NOTES

1   David Potter and Brian Harris discuss later in the book some of the problems that face Christians in these areas.

2   This distinction between word and act occurs elsewhere in Scripture. Proverbs 3:11 says, 'My son, despise not the *chastening* of the Lord; neither be weary of his *correction*.' Quoting this, the writer to the Hebrews has the same dual exhortation: 'My son, despise not thou the *chastening* of the Lord, nor faint when thou art *rebuked* of him' (Heb. 12:5; cf. also Rev. 3:19). Jay Adams has written extensively about the word of admonition in his books on nouthetic counselling.

FURTHER READING

[Much helpful writing is available on parenthood, as well as much that is less valuable. These suggestions are taken from easily accessible sources, and provide a starting-point from which readers will be able to find their own way. John White (*Parents in Pain*, Inter-Varsity Press, 1980) and D. M. Lloyd-Jones (*Life in the Spirit*, Banner of Truth, 1974, pp.235-302) cover extensive ground helpfully. Jay Adams' writing has been referred to already. His chapter on 'Discipline with Dignity' in *Christian Living in the Home* (Baker Book House, 1972) is the best starting-place for this subject. If you find workbooks fruitful, Wayne Mack has a constructive section in his *How to Develop Deep Unity in the Marriage Relationship* (Presbyterian & Reformed, 1977, Units 7 and 8).

The best all-round book for reading with little children is Marian Schoolland's *Leading Little Ones to God* (Banner of Truth, 1970). Children of junior school age cannot be introduced to anything better than Marianne Radius' books on the Old and New Testaments respectively (*Two Spies on a Rooftop*, Baker Book House, 1968, and *Ninety Story Sermons*, Baker Book House, 1966).

Editor]

4

Childhood and Adolescence

DAVID P. KINGDON

Childhood begins with birth into a family. Normally a family will comprise at least father, mother and child, and possibly other children as well.[1] In the society of biblical times, especially during the Old Testament era, the family unit would have been larger than this, including grandparents, uncles and aunts, cousins and so on. This is still the case in many parts of the world. For example, in most of Africa the extended family, as it is termed, is the norm, whereas the nuclear family of only father, mother and children, which is common in Western countries, is exceptional.

Childhood not only begins with birth into a family; it is also experienced within a family. For the family is the divinely ordained sphere of society for the upbringing of children (Gen. 1:27-28; 2:24; Eph. 6:1-4). Alan Stibbs succinctly states the biblical teaching: 'When God created man He made male and female, two in one; and He made them capable of giving birth to a third—the child; and indeed to several children—the family. Consequently it is in the context of a family that man is first born and reared, and later realizes natural human completion and fulfilment in marriage and parenthood.'[2]

Within the context of the Christian family a child should receive 'the training and instruction of the Lord' (Eph. 6:4). This will be both indirect and direct. For example, the child is indirectly furnished with a model of marriage as he experiences the love which exists between his father and mother in their marriage relationship, as it sets forth the relationship between Christ and His church (Eph. 5:22-33). Later, at the appropriate stage of the child's development, he can and should be given direct instruction about the marriage relationship. This will, of course, ring hollow if the child has already picked up the fact that there is tension in the marriage. 'Godly example' is therefore no cliché. It is the bedrock on which all direct training and instruction are built.

Training and instruction contain not only direct and indirect elements; they also combine both informal and formal components. This is clear from a brief study of Deuteronomy 6:6-9. According to the seventh verse each day is to begin and end with instruction. The ninth verse indicates that the commandments are to be given written as well as oral form, and displayed in prominent places where they can easily be seen (door-frames and gates). Here, then, is what might be termed formal instruction. However, during the course of the day opportunities will arise, both indoors and out of doors, for instruction in the law of God ('when you sit at home and when you walk along the road' v.7). In such circumstances instruction is given informally, involving no doubt the stimulating and answering of the child's questions (cf. Exod. 12:26-27). It is a Victorian idea, altogether without biblical authority, that children should be seen and not heard!

It is also clear from Deuteronomy 6:6-9 that a combination of informal and formal instruction serves the purpose of demonstrating to the child that biblical faith relates to the whole of life. There is no suggestion that between the instruction which begins and ends the day a surrender may take place to the secular, God and His Word being left out of account in facing the demands of daily living. The reverse is true. God and His Word come into every activity. The whole of life is to be consecrated to Him and ordered by His Word (Rom. 12:1-2). In our society this means in practical terms that a child is to be taught that he does household tasks, plays and learns to the glory of God (see 1 Cor. 10:31).

Presupposed in the Christian family is an authority structure, the existence of which will impinge upon the child's consciousness well before he or she becomes intellectually aware of it. Both parents, as believers, are in subjection to the Lord. The husband is the head of the wife, loving her and cherishing her as Christ does the church (Eph. 5:25,29). The wife submits to her husband as to the Lord (v.22). The child submits to both parents (Eph. 6:1-3).

As the child learns to obey within the authority structure of his home, he gradually becomes aware, as he develops in understanding, that there are other authority structures in society beyond his immediate family circle. There is the authority structure of teacher/child at school (to which our Lord's relationship to His disciples provides some analogy); that of employer/employee at work (see Eph. 6:5-9); that of the state/citizen (Rom. 13:1-7). As he first experiences the authority structure of his family, and is taught from the Bible about other such structures, so he is prepared for working life and responsible citizenship. Where, however, there is a widespread breakdown in family life, as there is today in the Western world, it is not surprising that the very fabric of society is under threat. For healthy economic and social structures depend ultimately upon healthy family structures.

BELIEVERS' CHILDREN

Up to this point I can, I think, presume upon the agreement of Bible-believing Christian parents. However, when we ask the fundamental question as to the spiritual status of a child born to Christian parents a sharp divergence of viewpoint becomes apparent.

Some Christian parents, generally [3] those who believe in the baptism of infants, maintain that their children are covenant children in virtue of their birth connection with their parents. They are therefore to be regarded as Christian children who can be expected to confirm their faith in later years when they are received into full church membership. On this view of the status of children born to Christian parents they will need only 'to be corrected by their parents and brought back to the Christian way from which they had strayed'.[4]

Other Christian parents, generally those who uphold believers' baptism, take a different view. They regard their children as non-Christians until such time as they are converted. They are in Adam until they are united to Christ by faith (Rom. 5:12; 1 Cor. 15:22). Birth connection with Christian parents is no ground for regarding a child as regenerate. Therefore the greatest need of the child is regeneration by the Holy Spirit.

If the first view of the child's status is adopted, parents will tend to regard their responsibility towards their children as pastoral and educational. They will see their task as being to teach their children that they are in the covenant and to encourage them to behave accordingly. If the second view is held, parents will see their responsibility primarily as evangelistic. They will thus call upon their children to repent and to place their trust in the Saviour of sinners.

Though I personally hold to the second view, I do not think that in practice there needs to be a sharp distinction between the pastoral and evangelistic approaches to the spiritual nurture of children. Parents who believe that their primary task is evangelistic do not, if they are wise, neglect to teach their children the ethical demands of the Christian faith. On the other hand, parents who regard their children as Christians in virtue of their covenant status pray that the fruits of regeneration may become apparent in the lives of their children. So both groups of parents in practice look for evidence of regeneration, which both recognize as the sovereign

63

and mysterious work of the Holy Spirit (John 3:8). Furthermore, both look forward to the day when each child shall come to the point of making a heartfelt and intelligent confession of faith, whether in the form of confirmation of some kind or in believers' baptism.

As they look back, parents whose children have come to the point of public confession of faith will see, if they reflect upon it, that the process of Christian nurture has been in fact a combination of evangelistic 'appeals' and pastoral training. The upbringing of the children of parents who do not regard them as covenant children has not been one long series of evangelistic exhortations. There has been teaching and training as well. On the other hand, parents who believe that their children are included within the covenant will, on a number of occasions, have pressed home the gospel demands of repentance and faith.

CHILDHOOD CONVERSION

That even little children can and do believe in the Saviour is clear. He Himself taught as much (Matt. 18:6). Yet childhood conversion is a subject surrounded with problems. Because this is so, Christian parents need great wisdom and discernment. They will often need to apply James 1:5 and fervently to pray that God will grant such wisdom.

Let us, then, notice some of the problems which arise in relation to childhood conversion. First, since a child usually (but not always!) wants to please his parents, he will say that he loves Jesus simply to gain their approval. So loving Jesus is seen as a way of gaining greater acceptance with father and mother. However, in later years it becomes obvious that the child's profession of faith was no more than a means to gaining the approval of his parents. Then the danger is that the parents will keep on insisting that the profession was real when the child knows that it was not.

Secondly, some children are much more pliant and conformist than others. Such children, like the chameleon, easily take their spiritual colour from their family environment. Yet in later years when, away from home, they are exposed to the ungodly surroundings of university or place of work, like the chameleon, they change their colour so as to merge into their new environment. Willingness to conform has led to adaptation to a new set of circumstances, and has shown that no true work of grace has taken place in the heart.

Thirdly, Christian parents need to be aware of the temptation to make their children conform to a certain type of conversion experience. The blinding conversion of Saul the Pharisee is hardly likely to provide the pattern for a young child being reared in a Christian home. Nor is that child likely to know the depth of conviction of sin which may be experienced by a converted drunkard.

The conversion of a child is frequently much more like the opening of a flower to the rays of the sun.[5] It is a process so gradual as to be almost imperceptible. Yet it is no less real than the conversion of a Saul. This needs to be emphasized because Christian children can hear or read testimonies of deliverance from gross sins, and almost be brought to the point of wishing that they could have committed such sins in order to be able to experience such deliverance. Clearly here is a new version of the old heresy of 'greater sinning, greater grace' (cf. Rom. 6:1-2).

Many Christians who have been reared in godly homes, when exposed to the insistence that there is only one kind of conversion experience—sudden, dramatic, and exuberant—have been given unnecessary anxiety of spirit. They almost come to regard their upbringing as a liability, depriving them of the kind of testimony they wish they could have had. Yet a godly upbringing is a very great privilege, and is probably the means God most uses in the increasing of His kingdom.

Anxiety can stem from another cause as well. When hearing a dramatic testimony with its sharp contrast between 'before' and 'after' (pre-conversion depravity and post-conversion joy), many a believer reared in a Christian home finds that it does not square with his experience. For him there is no such sharp contrast between 'before' and 'after', for the simple reason that for as long as he can remember he has always loved Jesus and trusted Him as Saviour. Is there something defective in his experience? No, not at all. To return to my analogy, he has always been opening to the sun of righteousness (Mal. 4:2). Why then should he be made to feel that he would have been spiritually better off if for a time he had been deliberately closed to the light of Christ?

Surely it would be better if the advantages of childhood conversion were more often taught from the pulpit. Conversion to the Saviour in childhood can save a life from many years wasted in the service of the world, the flesh and the devil. It can also save a person from forms of sin which leave lasting scars upon the conscience.

Parents would do well to exercise a wise caution when a child says that he 'has given his heart to Jesus'. On the one hand, the child should not be put on a pedestal. 'This is Tommy. He is six. He has given his heart to Jesus', a proud parent once said to me.

Tommy's chest, of course, swelled with pride! Pride, however, is not something that a true work of grace engenders in the heart.

On the other hand, at the opposite extreme, parents must not discourage a child by hinting that he is too young to come to Jesus. Our Lord spoke of little ones (*mikra*) who believe in Him. Fanny J. Crosby is reflecting our Lord's teaching in the words of one of her children's hymns:

> *We are little children,*
> *Very young indeed,*
> *But the Saviour's promise*
> *Each of us may plead.*
>
> *If we seek Him early,*
> *If we come today,*
> *We can be His little friends,*
> *He has said we may.*

One final point needs to be made in relation to conversion in childhood. Parents should not expect from a child who has professed conversion a level of understanding and a standard of behaviour that are beyond the level of his maturity. The apostle Paul had regretfully to treat the Corinthian believers as spiritual infants (1 Cor. 3:1-2). Parents should not make the mistake of treating Christian children as if they were grown-up in Christ. For if they have impossible expectations of them they will certainly exasperate them (Eph. 6:4; cf. Col. 3:21).

GROWING UP

As children develop and mature, so their relationship to their parents undergoes a subtle change. So long as they remain in the home they are under the authority of their parents. Biblically speaking, it is only when a man marries that a new authority structure is created. However, the relationship of children to parents is not static. It is dynamic and changing, for children grow from babyhood into boyhood or girlhood, and then on into their early teens when they are neither full-grown adults nor any longer children.

Christian parents need to recognize the changing nature of their relationship with their children as they grow to maturity; otherwise they are likely to exasperate them. Tommy at 16 resents being treated as if he were still mother's little boy. Mary reaches the stage at which she wants to choose her own clothes, not to have them chosen for her. Children do not stay dependent. They develop a sense of independence as they mature.

This being so, the authority of Christian parents needs to be wisely exercised. In the early stages of childhood reasons do not need to be given. A child must obey because mother or father says so. Reasons do, however, need to be given as children mature. Furthermore, parents need to have such an open relationship with their children that issues can be talked through calmly and thoughtfully. I am not suggesting that parents should abdicate their authority and allow their teenage children to do as they please. What I am arguing is that reasonable authority achieves far more than bare authority.

Parents ought not to feel threatened if they are sometimes questioned as to the validity of their views. They may conceivably lack biblical warrant, and it is not unknown for children to spot this! For instance, many Christian parents too often want for their children exactly what unbelieving parents want for theirs, especially that they 'get on' in life. They may find, however, that one or more of their children challenge them on biblical grounds. Is 'getting on' equivalent to loving God and neighbour? Surely not! If parents are wise they will examine the challenges to their thinking which their teenage children bring before them. They will not dismiss them out of hand and take refuge in their parental authority. Should their children be proved right, parents ought to be humble enough to thank them for showing them their error.

Nor, if parents are sensible, will they confuse matters of taste with the authority of clear biblical teaching. For example, whilst it is clear from Scripture that pre-marital sex is forbidden, it is by no means apparent that a pipe-organ is more sacred than a guitar, and that the one can be used in public worship and the other not. Nor is it obvious that non-manual work is more acceptable to God than manual work; yet this is the assumption that middle-class Christian parents often impose upon their children.

It is also important that parents should recognize that children differ as to their gifts. Out of three children in a family only one may be academically bright. It would be quite wrong if the other two were to be obliged to follow academic careers simply because their parents have academic backgrounds. Why should one not become a garage mechanic and another a nurse? Parents need to realize that on biblical grounds it is impossible to arrange work in a hierarchical order, in which manual work comes at the base of the pyramid. Our Lord was the 'son' of a carpenter, and a number of His first disciples were fishermen. I stress this point because I have known Christian parents provoke rebellion in a child through

67

forcing him to follow a career for which he was not equipped intellectually. The result has been disastrous. The child has come to reject the faith of his parents as well as their ambition for him.

Parents, of course, can and should guide their children in the choice of a career or calling. They can do this by helping to gather information about university or polytechnic courses, apprenticeships and so on. However, guidance is one thing, dictation is another. The choice of a career is in the end the choice of the child, not the choice of the parents.

Parents have a great responsibility today to help their children to resist peer group pressure. There is today a 'pop' sub-culture which is largely the creation of ungodly media and commercial interests. This spreads anti-Christian values among young people, who are subjected to enormous pressure to conform to the mores of their group. Christian homes ought to be producing young believers who are able to withstand the pressure of their peers in a principled fashion.

The only way in which this can be done is to encourage our teenage children in the habit of critical analysis based upon the Word of God. The young believer should be taught that he is in principle a nonconformist in his thinking. His renewed mind will not allow him to be conformed any longer to the pattern of this world (Rom. 12:2). It is part of his calling as a believer to test everything, hold on to the good, and to avoid every kind of evil (1 Thess. 4:21-22).

The development of a Christian mind is a two-way process. Parents need to be well-informed about the society in which they live, especially about the youth sub-culture. They should be able to talk intelligently about it, and avoid the temptation to dismiss all of it with a blanket condemnation. Teenagers need to be encouraged to talk to their parents about what is happening among their friends at school or at work. As parents and children talk together and seek to subject the matters they discuss to the scrutiny of Scripture, both will be strengthened to face the onslaughts which are being made today on Christian faith and morals.

Children can also be subjected to pressures within their families. Parents expect high standards of their children's school-work, but they also require them to attend so many meetings at their church that their school-work can suffer as a result. Or they are so concerned that their children achieve good results at school that they allow them to neglect services on the Lord's day. Parents need to sit down with their children and to define goals with them. Having done so, let them agree together on a programme which will allow the children to do justice to the often competing demands of home, school (or work) and church.

68

When young people leave home to study, to take up employment or to get married, they ought to feel that they can return with joy to find a listening ear, an encouraging word and sound Christian counsel. The last should be freely available without being forced upon them.

Young people for their part have a responsibility to keep in touch with their parents. They ought to be ready to help them as they get older. Home is not a hotel which can be left behind without a thought. Home is where a family has been lovingly and sacrificially reared. Sad it is when aging parents are neglected because their grown-up children are too wrapped up in their own affairs to bother about them.

As I write this chapter in Pretoria, South Africa, I can sum up what I have been trying to say in the words of a sampler which hangs on a wall of the house in which I am staying: 'There are two lasting gifts we can give to our children. One is roots, the other is wings.'

NOTES

1 I use the word 'normally' because, biblically speaking, it is doubtful whether one can describe a widowed mother of a young child as in a normal situation. Hence the emphasis of Scripture on the sorrow and difficulty of widowhood. Likewise it is questionable whether the common term 'single-parent families' should be used by Christians, the point being that this is an abnormal situation.

   That is not to suggest, of course, that God is not gracious to the widow or to the single parent. Scripture makes it abundantly clear that He is. But it is equally clear that there is real deprivation and loss to family life when one or both parents are not, for various reasons, involved in the upbringing of children.

2 A. M. Stibbs, *Family Life Today* (Appleford: Marcham Manor Press, n.d.), p.17.

3 The Southern Presbyterian (USA) theologians, Dabney and Thornwell, regarded baptized children as unregenerate covenant children until they gave evidence of regeneration. On this point see my *Children of Abraham* (Haywards Heath, Sussex: Carey Press, 1973), pp.62-64.

4 E. M. B. Green, *Evangelism in the Early Church* (London: Hodder & Stoughton, 1970), p.220.

5 I owe this analogy to the late Rev. W. G. Channon, with whom it was my privilege to serve as assistant at Banstead Road Baptist Church, Purley, Surrey, in the early 1960s.

FURTHER READING

Apart from books referred to in the text, the following are particularly helpful.

James Dobson, *Hide or Seek* (Hodder & Stoughton, 1982).
James Dobson, *Preparing For Adolescence* (Vision House, Santa Ana, California, 1978).
Martin E. Clark, *Choosing Your Career* (Presbyterian & Reformed, 1981).
John White, *Parents in Pain* (Inter-Varsity Press, 1980).

5

The Handicapped Child

DAVID C. POTTER

The prospect of parenthood is commonly a source of happiness among young couples. In the months of anticipation they plan for the event with some excitement, especially if it is to be their first child. There is so much to do, so many things to buy, and arrangements to be made for the confinement. Although they have some idea of when the child will be born, most cannot know with certainty, nor will they usually know whether their baby will be a boy or a girl.

Some expectant mothers, and even some fathers, are also apprehensive. They have a deep-seated fear that all may not be well for their child. This may arise from something in their family history—a record of physical deformity or mental handicap. More often than not it is an irrational fear. Frequently the mother's first question after the birth is, 'Is he/she all right?' Usually the answer is 'Yes!'—but not always.

The first reaction to the news that the new-born is handicapped will at best be disappointment, and at worst despair. Much will depend on how the parents are told the news, and much too will depend on how much they know about the particular handicap. Either way they will see their dreams and hopes tumble. Theirs will not be the typical TV family—even if mother is beautiful and father handsome. This little girl may have pretty blonde hair, but what of her deformed legs? This little boy may have a lovely personality, but what of the fact that he is mongol?

One sentiment will overwhelm all others—fear. They will be afraid not of the child as such, now so dependent and needy, but of the unknown and unknowable. There may be issues they must face immediately—an operation for an obstruction or a spinal lesion, or to rectify a cleft palate. They may even be offered a choice as to whether or not the child survives the first day or two of its life. A terrifying choice!

Beyond those early days is the clawing anxiety of the more distant future. I sat in the hospital ward with a young couple whose third baby, a boy, had Down's syndrome. They needed help in the face of what they saw as a deep disappointment. Two days had passed since the birth, but already the future loomed large for them. 'What will we do when he is 15 or 20?' It is a real fear for most parents of incurably handicapped children. Their early understandable ignorance makes them question whether they can cope with the as yet undiscovered problems which must surely be faced. 'Can they operate to help him? How badly retarded will he be? Will she need special treatment all her life? Will our marriage stand the strain?'

The fact of the matter is that one child in every hundred is born mentally handicapped,[1] and to that number must be added the many forms of physical handicap that may occur. So the possibility of a handicapped child being born into your immediate or extended family must be faced. And if you should be spared, many others will be afflicted, some of whom you may be in a position to help.

Many children become handicapped in early life. Although they come into the world as healthy infants, some illness or mishap in early years may distort the rest of their lives. Sometimes an injection intended to prevent illness goes sadly wrong, causing extensive brain damage. Sometimes a childish accident—which in most cases might bruise a knee or break an arm—causes severe injury resulting in permanent handicap. The disappointment is no less when such things happen, and the struggle to accept what has taken place may be even greater.

THE CHILD AND THE FAMILY

It is not only the child who is handicapped. There is a sense in which the whole family becomes handicapped. In almost every area of family life the presence of this special child will bring its own complications. It may mean the demands of prolonged incontinence, difficulties in the use of public transport, problems when shopping, disturbed nights, and so on.

The family members will not only struggle with the real difficulties of coping with the handicapped child. They will have the added burden of their own emotional adjustment to the problem. For all that they may agree with the idea that God is in charge of human affairs, they now have to live with a strange providence. The question will inevitably surface—'Why?' Why does God allow 'innocent babies' to be born handicapped? Why should this happen to 'good' people? Is this a judgment for past sins? Why should this happen to *me*? Only those who have not suffered would try to side-step such questions. They might reply, 'You must have faith.' To which the parent might reasonably respond, 'But I hurt!' Most people today consider health and happiness to be their right, and that includes having healthy, whole and, if possible, handsome children.

The Bible does not concur with this philosophy. It teaches that we live in a broken world where the consequences of sin are evident on every hand. It is the estrangement of people from God which is at the root of all human suffering. Prior to the disobedience of our common parents Adam and Eve, the world was perfect; no sin, pain or handicap was known. Since their 'fall' the whole world is disjointed, and everything in it is affected.

However, though God might justly have abandoned humanity to its fate, He has not done so. Indeed He now takes and uses the seeming tragedies to good purpose. He allows suffering as part of our human experience so that we may be developed as people—in character and in spirituality too. In God's hands hardship can have both a humbling and cleansing effect upon us. It brings a greater sense of need and more willing dependence upon God. It must be recognized *and* accepted that God is good and acts with good purpose in the lives of those who trust Him. That we cannot always understand the what, the why and the when does not alter this fact. If we take seriously God's own involvement in suffering to meet the greatest of human needs by providing a sin-bearer, then we cannot doubt that He will be concerned with our other pressing burdens also. The Bible puts it like this: 'He who did not spare his own Son, but gave him up for us all—how will he not also, along with him, graciously give us all things?' (Rom. 8:32).

Parents who find that God's blessings to them include a handicapped child must come to terms with this as part of God's providence. It is not a punishment, nor is it a 'cross'. It is the deliberate purpose of a loving heavenly Father. His grace is available to them in sufficient measure to support them in their need.

The grandparents may find it even more difficult than the parents to come to terms with the problem. They hope for the best for their children, and while they may cope with the fact that their son is made redundant or their daughter has difficulty in making ends meet, the painful reality of a handicapped grandchild is much harder to bear. They take a strange pride in the second generation, and this is inevitably marred by physical or mental defect.

Once again the issue must be faced in terms of the wisdom and providence of God. For the grandparent this ought to be easier. Longer life should lead to a wider experience of God's overruling strange and painful circumstances for good. But just as they may feel that 'it could never happen to me', so they may disregard the possibility of good coming from what seems evil. Grandparents too will need help.

Then there are the other children in the family. It is quite certain that their lives will be 'abnormal' in so far as the handicapped child will make demands on the family unit. If there are periods of hospitalization, the brothers and sisters may have to be looked after by dad or granny, while mum is away at the hospital. If the child is physically dependent, they may be limited in the range of places they can visit together and the types of activity in which the family may engage. Hill-walking is certainly not possible in a wheelchair!

The danger does exist, and must be guarded against, that they can be jealous of the more dependent family member, bitter at the extent to which they too are made to suffer, and resentful of the affection which might have been theirs. Vigilance by the parents and support from their friends can prevent this.

It is not all negative, however. They will also enjoy advantages denied to 'normal' families. With careful handling the parents can help them to adapt to their unusual circumstances in a way which will enrich their life-experience. They will be able to accept handicap far more happily than others in the community and will recognize the worth of those who are disabled. It is interesting to see how often children growing up with a handicapped person take up nursing, teaching, residential care work or social work among those who are handicapped.

THE CHILD AND THE FAMILY IN SOCIETY

One aspect of life in a handicapped family which is common to most, regardless of whether the problem is physical or mental disability, is isolation. Even in a society which is relatively compassionate, the presence of a handicapped person pushes his or her family to the fringes of their community, regardless of social standing. This is partly due to a widespread fear of the unknown. People ask questions like, 'Will this retarded child respond if I talk to him? Can that deformed boy understand what I am saying?' The classic example of this is when the parent is asked, 'Does he take sugar?', even though the handicapped person is well able to speak for himself. A young mother with a mongol child in a pushchair must grow used to the stares of passers-by.

The result of this apprehension is that the family tends to turn in on itself. Other children rarely come to play—either because they

74

or their parents are afraid that they 'might catch something', or because the other children are unkind to the handicapped person. It is unusual for the family to be asked out to tea, and even more unusual for the handicapped child to be asked out to tea alone. It is uncommon for the parents to go out together because few will offer to 'baby-sit' for them.

Another reason for the isolation is the assumption that any social problem with which we are not personally familiar is 'their' responsibility. 'They' should do something about it. 'They' are the Government, either local or national. It is what we have come to expect in a Welfare State. It is true that Health Authorities are responsible for the infirm, and that Social Services Departments care for the needy. But this assumption develops in society at large an unfortunate reaction—*I* have no responsibility for them. This overlooks the fact that state provision is often inadequate.

It is understandable that people are uncertain in the presence of what is unfamiliar. If you have never met a man in a wheelchair who has gained his Doctor of Philosophy degree, you may well assume that because a person cannot use his legs he cannot use his head either. If you have never romped on the carpet with a mentally handicapped child, you may imagine that such people are incapable of fun. What every person in society has to come to terms with is that a handicapped child is a real human being. He has as much right to be treated as an individual as anyone else. He has as much to contribute to the well-being of society as the rest of us, even though that may be in a different manner or at a different level. His place is not on the fringes of the community, isolated either physically or emotionally from everyone else, educated and cared for as if he were another species, perhaps of the animal kingdom. His place is among our children, within the social context of those who call themselves 'normal'.

This can be argued on humanitarian grounds, but if we shift the focus to the teaching of the Bible the rightness of the full acceptance of the handicapped person in society is even more plain. Scripture emphasizes that people are made in the image of God. It makes no exceptions on the grounds of ethnic origin, nationality, social background or handicap. The handicapped person is no less human than the able-bodied. It is the divine imprint that makes people special, and it is to be found also in those who are handicapped.

To accept this fact is to accept also that we have some responsibility for these people. The Bible lays strong emphasis on the duty of God's people towards those in need. The social life of Old Testament Israel was structured to accommodate the frail, the

75

elderly, the handicapped, the poor, the stranger and so on. Society today has an ongoing responsibility to care for the handicapped. It takes time and money to provide for them. Some will be able to live semi-independently if the extra support they need is forthcoming. If there is access for their wheelchair, or increased volume on their telephone, or housing suited to their requirements, or sheltered care, many can take their place among the rest of us on more or less equal terms. Some will need far more support, permanent care, special accommodation, nursing and medical supervision. But these extra requirements do not make them any less real people.

While they remain in the family unit the support and help will be required there. A full range of assistance should be available to them, from the level of a relatively undemanding encouragement by friendship through to the necessary physical provision for their special needs. These are our responsibilities. We actually elect 'them', those Members of Parliament or Councillors who spend our money in solving problems. We have the right, duty and power to influence what happens in our society.

Similarly we have responsibility at the more personal level. We live in the same street as the mentally handicapped, blind, deaf or physically handicapped child. The State may provide him with a school, or her with a wheelchair, but it has no monopoly on love, on personal interest and friendly help. There is more than sufficient room for us to make whatever practical contribution is within our scope.

THE CHILD, THE FAMILY, AND THE CHURCH

Ann's parents decided that it would be good for their daughter to go to Sunday school. They were not practising Christians themselves, but they were 'old-fashioned' enough to recognize the value of a spiritual dimension to life. However, Ann was a mentally handicapped child. They went to see the minister to make sure there would be no problems and were appalled at his response. The Sunday school could not accept her because it would be detrimental to the children of church members!

If it were unique it would be a grievous incident, but in fact it is less than rare. Even Christians who have had a handicapped child have found that their own church has been unfeeling and unhelpful towards them. The reverse ought to be the case. 'As we have opportunity, let us do good to all people, especially to those who belong to the family of believers' (Gal. 6:10).

Every Christian has a duty to love. It is not an option but an obligation. That love is first to be directed towards God and then to our neighbour. The first issue to face is just what the Bible means by love. In our sentimental age the very word is devalued either to mean a passing fancy or a sexual act. Not that this is very original. In New Testament days the church had to bring into play a word for love which was little used in society in order to express its distinctive understanding of love as an affectionate and practical concern.

Such love is very demanding, if it is in any way to reflect God's love for us. God's love cost Him nothing less than the life of His only Son. Our love is to reflect the same unselfishness, the same generosity, the same willingness to give even ourselves for the good of another person. John makes this point very clearly: 'This is how we know what love is: Jesus Christ laid down his life for us. And we ought to lay down our lives for our brothers. If anyone has material possessions and sees his brother in need but has no pity on him, how can the love of God be in him? Dear children, let us not love with words or tongue but with actions and in truth' (1 John 3:16-18).

The question may arise as to whom we are to love in this way. When told to love his neighbour, a lawyer raised the same issue — 'Who is my neighbour?' Jesus replied by telling the parable of the Good Samaritan (Luke 10:29-37). Its point is that the person in need is our neighbour — regardless of race, religion or colour. No matter what the potential danger or inconvenience to us, we are to show practical and affectionate concern for him and to do for him what we would have wanted him to do for us if the circumstances were reversed.

Now bring this back to the matter in hand. Here is a family with a handicapped child. They are a part of your church family, part of the body of Christ. The particular needs they have will vary from case to case, but that they have needs is obvious even to the most casual observer. How will you respond to those needs? You have two options. You may treat them as the poor, cold visitor was treated. 'Suppose a brother or sister is without clothes and daily food. If one of you says to him, "Go, I wish you well; keep warm and well-fed," but does nothing about his physical needs, what good is it?' (James 2:15-16). Alternatively, you may show a real concern to help them.

Be interested in them as a family. Perhaps there will be extra visits to hospitals or clinics when they need transport. It will be a shame if they have to order a taxi. Perhaps their other children will have to be met from school and given tea. What a pity if it is left to non-Christian neighbours to offer help. There may be some special piece of equipment which would help so much but cannot be provided by the National Health Service. The Rotary Club might offer, but how much better if the church does so!

If the handicapped person has to use a wheelchair, it may be that your church is the last place he can visit. Our nonconformist chapels frequently boast a flight of steps up to the main entrance, and another flight down to the narrow-door toilets! One Baptist church in London has two 'wheelchair stewards' to carry the handicapped person and chair into the building. A removable ramp may be provided. Once inside it may be necessary to shorten a pew so that the wheelchair does not block the aisle. If a church is unsure how best to help, let them ask the family, or the handicapped person concerned.

There is also a large gospel opportunity to be taken among non-Christian families with handicapped children. So few step over their gulf of isolation. If Christians do so they may find an initial reserve bordering on suspicion, especially if the help is felt to be conditional—'You come to church and I will help you'. But if there is perseverance and genuine love it may well win the family. On the other hand the response may be of glad surprise that someone has shown that they care. One father of a mentally handicapped girl was converted because Christians offered to take his daughter to Sunday school. He went too, and heard the gospel for the first time in his life.

For those who know Jesus Christ as Saviour there is one door that is firmly closed to them—that of rejecting the handicapped child. In a society which is increasingly ready to dispose of the subnormal or the abnormal, it is the responsibility of Christians to receive them in the name of Christ and to show practical love for them and their families.

There is the opportunity to present the gospel to the handicapped person also. A distorted body or a limited mind does not render a person incapable of salvation! Regeneration is a miracle whenever it happens, whether to the clever or to the blatantly wicked. Many Christians assume that the mentally handicapped person is incapable of responding to the gospel. This says a good deal about our view of conversion as a largely intellectual process. In fact, it is by the power of God's Spirit that a person is made new in Christ, and He is able to work regardless of the presence or absence of natural ability. Remember that Jesus said, 'I praise you, Father, Lord of heaven and earth, because you have hidden these things from the wise and learned and revealed them to little children. Yes, Father, for this was your good pleasure' (Luke 10:21).

NOTES

1 This rule of thumb figure is used by many organizations working with the mentally handicapped. Estimates of severely mentally handicapped children suggest about 3.6 in every 1,000 live births.

FURTHER READING

Christians have written little which deals directly with mental or physical handicap. This is not to say that helpful literature does not exist. Christians may often be helped by books that deal with the great principles of biblical teaching. Joni Eareckson has said, 'Without a doubt, what helps us most in accepting and dealing with suffering is an adequate view of God' (*A Step Further*, Pickering & Inglis, 1979). Thus, J. I. Packer's *Knowing God* (Hodder & Stoughton, 1975), or D. M. Lloyd-Jones, *Faith on Trial* (Inter-Varsity Press, 1965), are of particular value. Some books on suffering include helpful discussions of handicap. Herbert Carson's *Facing Suffering*, chapter ten (Evangelical Press, 1978), and Peter Jeffery, *Our Present Sufferings* (Evangelical Press of Wales, 1982) are just two examples. Slightly differently, Susan Macaulay's *Something Beautiful from God* (Marshall, Morgan & Scott, 1980) has a helpful section entitled 'When Something Goes Wrong'.

Joni Eareckson's testimony of how she faced disability is strongly recommended (*Joni*, Pickering & Inglis, 1978). The cassette, *Suffering*, produced by the Strict Baptist Mission, 12 Abbey Close, Abingdon, OX14 3JD, also includes helpful testimonies. The Christian Medical Fellowship has produced one of the few books on handicap (*God and the Handicapped Child*, 1982), although it is not written in a popular style. Pastors and others called on to counsel the handicapped will find it helpful to consult Jay Adams' brief chapter, 'Counselling the Disabled', in his *Update on Christian Counselling*, Volume II (Presbyterian & Reformed, 1981). Presenting the gospel to the handicapped is touched on briefly in this chapter. For a fuller discussion, refer to the cassette, *Communicating the Gospel to the Handicapped*, by David Potter, obtainable from the Association of Christian Teachers, Stapleford House, Wesley Place, Stapleford, Nottingham, NG9 8PD. Finally, David Potter's *Too Soon to Die* discusses one of the questions frequently facing the parents of handicapped children, that of euthanasia (Evangelical Press, 1982).

6

Fostering and Adoption

STUART OLYOTT

Befriending other people's children is a Christian duty. The Word of God instructs us to be like our Saviour. It was somebody else's boy that He held in His arms that day in Galilee (Mark 9:36). The 12-year-old girl whose hand He held, and whose supper He organized, was somebody else's daughter (Mark 5:41-43). It was other people's children that He blessed, and insisted on receiving, despite the disapproval of the disciples (Matt. 19:13-15). He watched other people's children at play (Luke 7:32), and always spoke of children with respect. He was the Friend of children, and no one is Christlike who is anything less.

You can start befriending other people's children before you ever get round to thinking about fostering and adoption. Consistent Christians kick a football with the lads of the neighbourhood, chat to the girls on the corner, take on holiday the child who never goes away, and frequently have other children sitting round their table and playing on their floor. Christian men befriend the boy who is being brought up by his mother, and Christian women spend an evening with those girls who only have a father—teaching them to sew and cook, and doing their hair, and seeing them to bed—while their dad has a break, and the opportunity to have an evening out.

It is humbug to think about fostering and adoption without being a friend of children first. This is because a Christian approach to this subject is built upon two simple convictions. The first is that other people's children matter as much as our own. Before we have other children permanently into our home, it needs to be seen that this basic conviction is more than an empty theory, but a principle by which we already live. The second conviction is that *all* children should be brought up in the love and security of a family.

But thousands of them are not. Our chapter is not long enough to go into all the reasons for this. Suffice it to say that very large numbers of boys and girls are having little or no experience of the family life God intended for them. A few of them are babies. Many more of them are handicapped, of mixed race, or belong to a minority ethnic group. Lots of them are teenagers. But the greatest proportion are children in the 7-12 age bracket, of whom the majority are boys. These children are growing up exactly where the Word of God says they should *not* be growing up, while at the same time thousands of Christian homes have a bed to spare, and do nothing about it. Is this loving our neighbour as ourselves?

FOSTERING: WHERE TO START

Not all fostering starts by an approach to the official channels. If you become a true friend to local children, many of them will come to you with their most intimate problems. In our own case this led to some of them coming to stay with us for shorter or longer periods, and a number of them for ever. This happened because in their cases it was the best solution to their particular problems. It was usually done with the approval and co-operation of their original families, and always with the knowledge of the local authority. The law in the United Kingdom is quite plain. The local authority must be informed of any child who lives with you for more than two weeks, unless that child is a relative. We knew that the law was as much for our benefit as for the child's. After all, who wants to be accused of kidnapping?

However, we admit that it is more normal for boys and girls to enter a new family in a more orthodox fashion. Most local authorities are looking for foster-parents, and if you thought you could extend your ministry of friendship to other people's children in this way they would be delighted to send round a social worker to discuss the subject with you. Such a visit would not commit either you or the local authority to anything, but would give you all the facts so that, as husband and wife, you could discuss the possibility more fully.

That might be the end of the matter for you. Or it might just be the beginning. If you decided to go ahead, and to offer your-selves formally as foster-parents, you would need to have some reasonable idea of what you were offering. What age of child would you prefer, and of what sex? Are you thinking of offering him a place in your family for a short period (because this is precisely the need of so many children, and, besides, the gifts of some couples are more suited to this); or were you thinking in terms of long-term, or permanent, care? You would also need to sit down and think through very seriously again what you are doing. You are not offering a child a *home*—that is something we do to kittens and puppies. You are offering him *a place in the family*. There are a million miles between these concepts, and the couple who cannot distinguish them is about to embark on a voyage where they are certain to be shipwrecked.

Once the local authority has received your formal application, it will want to ask you a hundred questions of its own, many of which will be exceedingly frank. These will range from details of your income and how you use your leisure to, if need be, the very personal question as to why you have no children of your own. Questions on your faith are inevitable, especially in this day of so many weird sects, and you will need to have thought out in advance how you can answer mildly, and yet without compromise. The Home Office Boarding Out Regulations, which govern fostering arrangements, state that 'Where possible a child shall be boarded out with foster-parents who either are of the same religious persuasion as the child or give an undertaking that he will be brought up in that religious persuasion.' The explanatory memorandum adds that, where practicable, an appropriate minister of the child's religious persuasion should be consulted before a child is fostered with people who are of a different religion.

We have often discussed the question of religious upbringing with social workers, as all our lads have been officially either Church of England or Roman Catholic. We have simply explained that our own church is an orthodox Protestant church where a quarter of the members and half the young people come from Roman Catholic homes. We have explained that there are certain things we do as a family, and going to church *as a family* is one of them. Would it not seem rather bizarre if one member went elsewhere? We have explained that, as the original parents were not practising, it is unlikely that they would mind—and all our own family were happy at the church, so it is unlikely that the child will mind either. After that there was never any difficulty. Most social workers of our acquaintance think that as long as there is some orthodox church observance, the terms of the law can be regarded as being observed, at least in spirit. But we have always been open with them at this point, and would counsel against anything which is devious.

Some social workers will be particularly interested to know your views on discipline, and not a few potential Christian foster-parents have been turned down at this point. We know, because it once happened to us. Our disappointment was profound, but under-girding us was the knowledge that God's providence rules the world, and that even this was in His will. A year later the local authority changed its mind, and apologized for misjudging us! We would counsel Christian couples to be entirely open with social workers, to hide nothing, and with sweet reasonableness to hold to what God's Word shows them to be right. Never do deals with social workers which will keep you from a full obedience to the will of God. We want to welcome boys and girls into a full-blooded Christian family life, not into an anaemic version of the real thing, emasculated by the Freudian dictates of a Social Services Department.

THE CHILD JOINS YOUR FAMILY

If you are approved as foster-parents, the time will come when you and a particular child will be put in touch with each other. How this is done will be governed by the particular needs and character of the child. A child who is to be with you for only three weeks, while his mother is in hospital, is a very different case from the youngster for whom permanent substitute parents are being sought. The first can be delivered to your door without notice, and told that this is where his home will be for a short while. No long-term relationship is envisaged. In the second case the child and the couple are usually introduced to each other over a period of time. The friendship starts with visits, then days out, weekends, and longer stays. It is only when a definite bond of affection and trust has been formed that the child moves in permanently. But even in these cases there are exceptions. Obviously each child is different, and there can be no set rules about bringing him and his new family together. It is something that has to be thought through by all the parties involved.

However, this much is certain. Even the child who comes 'for keeps' is, in his own mind, only 'giving it a try'. He is there to see if the relationship will work out. But you are not. When you first made contact with him, it was with the probability of having him as a member of your family. From the moment he steps through your door, that is exactly what he is. Whatever may be the thoughts in his own mind, and whatever may be the legalities of his particular case, every day he is in your home he is as much a full member of the family as if he had been born there. It will never be *you* who take the initiative that he should leave. The law may require it, the social workers may arrange it, or it may even be requested by the child himself. But such an idea will never come from *you*. My wife and I feel that we cannot stress this point too much. *Unreserved acceptance* is fundamental to any Christian approach to fostering.

Only bad parents show their dependent children the door. We are children of God, and very poor ones at that. We rebel, misbehave, and are so often slow to understand. We disobey, are ungrateful, and repeatedly manifest the habits we had before we entered the divine family. But our Father remains our Father who, in His limitless tenderness, provides for our needs and chastens us for our profit. All fatherhood must take His fatherhood as its example, and all family life must be based on the principles which operate in His family. Whatever this child does—*whatever*—we will never show him the door, discuss alternative arrangements with him, or even mention the possibility. Nor will we even entertain it in our hearts. Whoever else has let him down, and however much *he* lets *us* down, we will never let *him* down. Never.

Whether this child is very small, or a teenager, he comes to you with at least part of his character already formed. He has his background, his habits, his way of doing things, and his own likes and dislikes. Little by little you are going to tackle these things. Much of what he says and does you will have to reject categorically. But you will never reject *him*. Family life is more than living in a house with parents. It is being accepted, *come what may*. Nobody has ever truly welcomed a child into their family who does not give him exactly the same status as those who are born there. You do not threaten your own children with 'sending them back', or use other patronizing language. The same must always apply to 'ready-made' children. *Unreserved acceptance* is at the root of a Christian approach to fostering, and every fostering breakdown that we ourselves know has been caused by the lack of it.

A NORMAL FAMILY LIFE

No child is enjoying unreserved acceptance who is being treated as special. Unfortunately even the best of social workers do not always see this clearly. With the highest of intentions they run all sorts of special treats for the foster-children of the neighbourhood, and these serve as a pleasant reminder to the child that he is not like other children. He is different. He is getting the treat because he is 'fostered'. Such treats are also divisive of the family life that you are trying to build, because not all the children in your family have the right to go to them. Not only so, but those who are left at home that day are regarded as more 'in' than the others—the very thing which a Christian view of total acceptance is trying to avoid.

We have tried to preserve our children from such treats, and social workers have generally understood why when the reasons have been explained to them. For ourselves, we regard all social workers as friends *of the family*, who can call when they like, and not as professionals who have only an interest in one or two members in particular. We encourage them to pop in when they please, to have meals with us whenever possible, and to ask as many straight questions as they want. We are naturally careful to ensure that they have time to be alone with the particular child for whom they are legally responsible. We do not allow our children to refer to 'my social worker' (or 'me welfare', as is common in Liverpool!), but insist that they always refer to them by their name. Our aim throughout is to make it easy for the social workers to do their job, while keeping our family life as normal as possible. We are not an institution, we are a family. Sometimes social workers seem to overlook this, and we need to speak to them frankly about anything they do which affects the 'family-ness' of our home. After all, even from their point of view, is not the whole purpose of fostering to give a child a family life *as near as possible to the real thing?* Fortunately it is not hard to be frank with friends.

But of course we must not live in a world of unreality. We know that our family has come about in a rather unusual way, and we feel strongly that there should be open and free conversation on this point whenever a child wants it. Not all of our youngsters have wanted to talk about themselves before the others, but all have felt the need fairly often to get certain things off their chest. For this reason we try to spend at least some time alone with each child every day, usually at bedtime. Like all people, children have a right to privacy, and we do not believe in prying questions. But where there is a spirit of trust, and a ready ear, a child will often reveal his heart of hearts, and fall asleep with a sigh of relief. Usually that is all that is necessary, though occasionally some action has needed to be taken in the light of the information given. These bedtime chats mean that a child's individual difficulties can be dealt with without there being any practical difference in the way that he is treated in the family. Not every bedtime chat has the same content, but every child gets one, and in this way impartiality in the family is preserved.

A greater difficulty may be created by a child's contact with his natural family. Our general experience is that such contact is always upsetting to the child—perhaps because he is looking forward to his return home (as with children in short-term care); or because he does not want anything to do with his original family (as when a child has been maltreated, for example); or, in perhaps the majority of cases, because he just does not know where he is. It is obvious that no simple rules can be given with respect to parental visits and contact with other relatives. This is an area where you will need considerable wisdom, and an excellent liaison with the social worker.

We would insist that no child should be able to come home from school to a situation for which he has not been prepared, and which he might find difficult to face. Our normal rule is that we have allowed no parent or other relative to call at our home unless this has been previously arranged. In difficult situations we have insisted that such arrangements should not be made directly, but with the social worker. In trying to give a child as normal a family life as possible, we must protect him from surprises of the traumatic variety.

Equally, when the child is out for the day, or away, with members of his original family, we must not give him the impression that he is being in any way disloyal to us. Most fostering, quite rightly, aims to reintegrate the child with his original family as soon as it is feasible. But neither must we give him the impression that he means anything *less* to us because of this family contact. It is important to keep him fully in the picture about all that has happened in his absence, so that he does not feel that he has 'missed out'. In turn, he will probably talk about his own activities during the visit. By this sort of communication the trust between us and the child continues, and we remain in a position to help him.

It also needs saying that when a child we love is spending the day with people we hardly know, or may have good reason to mistrust, we ourselves are likely to have an overwhelming sense of personal insecurity. Once more it is time to recall that we can trust the providence of God. He really is working out things for our good. This is also the time to pray in a special way for the child, particularly if he is having a difficult time, or the visit in question is likely to have a bearing on decisions made about his future. But the child must never see our sense of insecurity. To him, we must be always the same. He must know that he has a pillar, and that whoever else lets him down, *we* will not.

SHALL WE ADOPT HIM?

The question of adoption does not arise until a child has been a member of our family for some time. British law is clear. You cannot adopt a child that you do not know. He must have been living with you for at least a few months first. But with such a child the question eventually arises naturally. This child is, to all intents and purposes, a member of our family. Shall we now try and get this *fact* recognized in *law?* [1]

The only consideration that we can honourably entertain in our minds at this point is the welfare of the child. Would it be for his good? And if so, is it something that the child himself wants? These two questions are primordial, and are also the two questions which most interest the law. It is simply a fact that some children do not need adopting, and that some of those who do, do not want it. If a child is old enough to express his own mind, no court in the land will require him to be adopted against his wishes. Nor will it grant an adoption order unless it is obviously to the child's advantage. It is plain that no one should try to adopt a child without careful thought and prayer beforehand.

Once these cautions have been heeded, we believe that Christians should be generally enthusiastic about adoption. After all, adoption is a biblical concept which expresses our own highest privilege. God does not just treat us in a fatherly way. He *is* our Father, and we are His children by faith in Jesus Christ. Adoption expresses, more than any other word, that we *belong* to God. We are His heirs and sons, and have all the rights and privileges of the children of God. And we are such children because we have been *chosen* to be. What a privilege!

This glorious biblical concept was built upon a human practice current in New Testament times. Our present practice is not identical to that which obtained in the first-century world, but is very similar to it. The children we have welcomed into our family can become legally ours. They can carry our name, and come to enjoy a perfectly ordinary family life, without the distraction of visits from social workers, regular medical examinations, and all the other paraphernalia of being 'in care'. We can give this child a greater security than that enjoyed by those born to us. In their case, we had to put up with whatever we got! But we have chosen this child, knowing full well what he is, and he has chosen us. These choices are now legally and finally settled in an adoption order.

Adoption brings some new problems, but in comparison with the advantages they seem very small. The family income drops when the local authority's boarding-out payments stop; but this is offset a little by the fact that you can now claim family allowance, or perhaps guardian's allowance. If you had a particularly good social worker, you may well miss her advice and support—though there is no reason at all why she should not continue to be the friend of the family that you have always regarded her to be. The child has the difficulty of using a new name at school, and for a little while may have new self-questionings about his identity. But once these difficulties have been surmounted, the child has what he has never had before. He has the opportunity of having an entirely normal existence—as normal as that of any friend in his class. He is a member of a family, and this now even the law recognizes. He need never nurse again the fear that perhaps someone will come along and end it all.

How to go about an adoption is beyond the scope of this chapter. It is an area where God's providence has given us a good deal of experience, and my wife and I would always be happy to write personally to any reader who would like to know more about this subject.[2] The same goes for anything else on which this chapter has touched. We would simply urge that couples who are sure that adoption is best for a child they have welcomed into their family should not be discouraged by the seemingly insurmountable difficulties that sometimes crop up. We have always acted on the principle that we should do what is right, not what is feasible. Difficulties fall before prayer and persistence! We have children who are enjoying the security of family life, who have been adopted against the advice of the local authority and without the consent of one natural parent. It is not normally as difficult as that, but, when it is, every obstacle and frustration is worth while, so that a child can have what he himself wants, and what God wants for him—an uncontested place in the family.

You will have noticed that this section seems to imply that the child being adopted is not a baby. This is the way it is today. Although a substantial proportion of children placed for adoption are still very young, the destruction of babies by abortion, and social trends in general, mean that there are currently far fewer babies available for adoption. But, as we have already said, there is no shortage of older children without a place in a family. We are called to answer the needs that actually exist, not the needs that we would prefer to exist. Who will receive one such child in the name of Christ?

TWO SORTS OF TEARS

In closing, it needs to be underlined that no child who enters your family will automatically become a Christian. This is true of those born into it, and even more true of those who join it later. This is because they come to you with their characters well formed. Before you sow your first grain of wheat, the devil has already sown ten thousand tares. You are not only working against inbred sin, but also often against an active antipathy to the things of God which they have imbibed from elsewhere. What tears we shed when those we love do not know the Saviour!

Your tears will flow faster when some of the children who have become members of your family one day cut the link with you, treat you as if they have never known you, go in search of relatives whose love is more imagined than real, and leave you nothing but the memory of their laughter in your home. You will feel that the grief is greater than you can bear.

The present adoption law allows that adopted children over the age of 18 should be provided with a copy of their birth record on application. For children placed before 1975, access to such records is not allowed without the child having an interview with a social worker, but if he insists, everyone must allow him to go ahead. Our own advice would be that Christian parents should not resist the youngster at this point. Tell him that it is perfectly natural that he should want to know about his original parentage; he would be funny if he never wondered about it. It is vitally important that the young person should not feel guilty or disloyal about wanting such information. If we ourselves have the information, and they really want it, we should give it to them. In this way we show how we understand them, and build yet one more bridge into their lives, rather than precipitating a conflict, and almost driving them to choose between us and their original families. None the less, we consider it important to explain a few things to the youngster before he gets the information he seeks. The facts that he finds out may not all be pleasant. His original parents may be very different from the people of his imagination, and he must be prepared for awful disappointments. He must also be prepared for some personal insecurity, because he will not be able to avoid feeling torn between two families; he may feel bitter towards his original parents, or he may start wondering whether he is, after all, a *full* member of his adoptive family. When our own boys did not have the information they wanted, we were always in a position to give it to them, and did so.[3] They were grateful, and in *their* cases this was enough. None of them ever went to visit or to look for his original parents.

If they do cut their links with you, the temptation will be to chase after them, to hunt them down, to accuse them of being ungrateful for all that you have done for them, and to cry 'I don't understand'. Resist the temptation, and walk the way of love. Now is the time to be the waiting father—to pray, to wait, to hope, to look to the horizon—but never to condemn. Another Father once did that for us, and we came home. When the gilt wears off the gingerbread, who wants to confess his folly to a patronizing nag? Wait, watch and pray, and the absent voice will one day call you again 'Mum and Dad'. And then a different sort of tear will flow.

In addition, we should remember that when we sow divine seed, some of it always grows. Not all of it, but some. Perhaps some youngsters in your family will come to Christ when they are young.

Who knows how God will work? Another will bitterly fight his Maker for many years, and then, when he has resisted Him all he can, will yield to a Lord and a Saviour. How much the Master loved him through all those difficult years! Let us follow more closely Him who loves and loves and loves and never gives up. What a joy it will be to know that the narrow door of our house has been for one boy or girl the narrow door that at last led to life! Such a fact humbles us even further before our heavenly Father, and causes that special sort of tear to sting our cheeks afresh.

NOTES

1 Most people plan either to foster or adopt, and the children come to their home clearly identified as foster-children or potential adopted children. In these cases, the experience of adoption will be different from our own.

2 Pastor Olyott's address is Route Du Signal 12, Ch—1018 Lausanne, Suisse.

3 We have always retained a copy of the child's birth certificate at the time of adoption in case the child should want, at a later date, to know some details about himself. When parents are dead we have obtained copies of their death certificates, so that we could furnish minimal details on that point too, without feeling that we were obliged to give them permanent 'mementos' of their previous family, unless they request them.

FURTHER READING

Very little has been written about fostering or adoption from a Christian standpoint. This is partly explained, in the case of fostering at least, by the fact that fostering only developed on a large scale in this century.

If you are considering caring for someone else's child, the British Association for Adoption and Fostering (BAAF) publishes a wide selection of practical literature, from books to leaflets (11 Southwark Street, London SE1).

Greg and Cathie Bahnsen, 'Adoption: Theological Treasure and Model for the Home' (*Journal of Christian Reconstruction*, Vol. 4:2, 1977), was written for an American audience, but is worth reading.

Christians of earlier generations usually thought in terms of residential care, and the zeal and concern of people like Francke, Müller, Spurgeon and Whitefield have much to teach us, even if we decide to pursue different avenues today. A number of articles by the editor are still available on Francke (*Banner of Truth*, 142, July

1975), Spurgeon (*Christian Graduate*, 29:3, Sept. 1976) and Whitefield (*Reformation Today*, 32, July 1976).

7

The Elderly and the Church

IAN SHAW

Our churches fail our old people. Partly as a result of this, they fail us. These twin convictions lie behind this chapter.

Evangelical Christians have shown a resurgent interest in social issues. Yet despite this, the place of the elderly in the family and the church has been largely ignored.

Shakespeare viewed the seventh age of man with bleak pessimism as

second childishness and mere oblivion;
Sans teeth, sans eyes, sans taste, sans everything.

This is a portrait of old age without society and without family; more seriously, of old age without God and without hope in the world. The Christian must have more to say, both to fellow believers and to those outside Christ.

GROWING OLD

Why does old age exist? In the last analysis, the answer is sin. Adam was told, 'When you eat of [that tree] you will surely die' (Gen. 2:17), and from the moment of eating the aging process began, the outward evidence of the inward curse of sin. Man became, as John Blanchard aptly remarks, 'a dead soul in a dying body'. Thus the natural body, whatever passing glories it may seem to have in its youth, is perishable, dishonourable and weak (1 Cor. 15:42-43).

Every society recognizes a category of people who are 'old', and it is generally true that women outlive men. Old age is always marked by some kind of formal or informal retirement, and most societies recognize that adult children have obligations to their elderly parents. Another general characteristic is the way in which life is valued and attempts are made to prolong it.

A truly biblical position requires recognition of the particular characteristics of old age in our own society and the application of

93

scriptural principles. With the improvement of health and medical standards, old age comes later in modern society. With increasing modernization, the proportion of elderly people in society increases, and a higher proportion live in cities. Modernization also tends to pull the extended family apart, and this brings a declining respect for the elderly and a loosening of the ties of obligation. The result is that the position of the elderly is undermined. Increased social and geographical movement weakens family bonds, and the net result is that responsibility for providing economic security for the elderly shifts to the State. In addition, rapid social change renders obsolete the hard-won skills and knowledge of the old. Younger people are often better educated, and the old cannot practise or teach others. An obvious illustration of this is the difficult position faced by some older pastors in rapidly developing countries.

Some of the evidence for these points has been given in the introductory chapter—the enormous increase in the proportion of elderly people during this century; the continuing increase in the relative numbers of elderly people over the age of 75; the implications of these developments for the family life of old people, particularly women. It is known that 45 per cent of elderly women over the age of 65 are living on their own.

A note of caution needs to be sounded at this point. We should beware of the romantic belief that the elderly are always neglected in our society, and that they were always cared for in the simpler, far-off days. There are two sides to many developments. For example, the extremes of poverty have gone. The elderly often feel that the attendant disciplines of making your own amusements and not taking things for granted were of profound value. Yet they would not want to return to poverty.

The difficulties are there. We must not underestimate them. Hearing and sight may diminish; memory becomes selective or deceptive. Certain illnesses are associated with old age; retirement has to be coped with, and there may be past regrets, loneliness, bereavement, poverty and loss of independence.

The Christian, however, should not fear old age. Old age, as one elderly Christian has recently written, is to be enjoyed. More precisely, we need to grasp afresh the realization that old age for the believer is intended by God to be a period of spiritual blessing and growth. Indeed, Scripture often enforces the truth that it is in the very context of physical weakness that spiritual strength is evidenced. Why did Paul delight in weaknesses? Because Christ's power was made perfect in weakness. Jacob learned the same lesson from wrestling with God at Peniel.

Contented now upon my thigh
I halt, till life's short journey end;
All helplessness, all weakness, I
On Thee alone for strength depend;
Nor have I power from Thee to move:
Thy nature and Thy Name is Love.

Lame as I am, I take the prey,
Hell, earth, and sin with ease o'ercome;
I leap for joy, pursue my way,
And as a bounding hart fly home,
Through all eternity to prove
Thy nature and Thy Name is Love.

Charles Wesley

It is surprising how rarely increasing age brings a corresponding increase in awareness of eternity. As one widow remarked, 'You won't believe this, but it just never occurred to us that one of us might die.' But are you a real Christian? There will come a day when aging will hinder communication and thought. 'Old age, with all its train and retinue of weakness and infirmities, will come. But if it bends thy back, do not keep thine iniquities to break it' (Charles Bridges).

What help, then, does Scripture give us on the particular questions posed by old age? A great deal if we are prepared to dig around for it. In the remainder of this chapter we shall be looking at what the Bible has to say from two points of view. First, what does it have to say to elderly people themselves? Broadly speaking, Scripture speaks by way of warning regarding the spiritual frailties of old age, and by way of exhortation and encouragement regarding the gifts and graces of believers grown old in years. Second, what does God have to say through the Scriptures to believers, as members of families and churches, about their responsibilities to and relationship with the elderly?

SPIRITUAL FRAILTIES OF OLD AGE

The elderly are taught and warned about a number of characteristic spiritual pitfalls of old age. These may be summarized as vain regrets, fear of the future, nostalgia, pride, and loss of spiritual vigour.

Vain regrets

Conscious of the uncertainties of life (e.g. Ps. 90) and one's own sinful failings, the old person may engage in unprofitable self-recrimination about sins committed, opportunities neglected, time wasted, etc. None of us is free from such failings, and we may fear that God will forsake us (Ps. 71:9). We are to grasp the scripture promise, 'I will restore to you the years the locust has eaten' (Joel 2:25). Paul was sadly aware of his life before his conversion as 'a blasphemer and a persecutor and a violent man', yet he was not discouraged. Rather he says, 'Forgetting what is behind and straining towards what is ahead, I press on towards the goal' (1 Tim. 1:13; Phil. 3:13-14).

Fear of the future

An undue preoccupation with the present often betrays a fear of the future. We realize how fleeting life is, that 'Man is a mere phantom as he goes to and fro' (Ps. 39:6). Yet we should strive to avoid the impression sometimes given in our prayer meetings, that the physical health of elderly people in the congregation is more important than their spiritual health.

This concern with the future also reveals itself in an increased preoccupation with material security. Archibald Alexander remarks 'how strange it is that the nearer men come to the end of their journey, the greater concern they feel as to the means of future subsistence'. Easy condemnation must be avoided. Old age is a time of greater poverty than most other periods of life. Yet how sad it is to hear sometimes of comparatively wealthy older Christians who seem to cling to their possessions when they could be of great help to their family or church. Barzillai is to be our example in this respect, who used his wealth wisely and generously and not for hope of reward (2 Sam. 17:27-29; 19:32ff.). Such generosity can be an encouragement to other believers far beyond the donor's realization. The service of Barzillai and his family was an encouragement to David on his own deathbed (1 Kgs. 2:7).

Nostalgia

'Do not say, "Why were the old days better than these?" For it is not wise to ask such questions' (Eccles. 7:10). The spiritual realism of Scripture recognizes that nostalgia can be one of the most insidious temptations faced by the old, partly because it may have some good mixed in with it, partly because it is such a commonly accepted characteristic of old age, and partly because it may have such damaging effects on other Christians.

I do not want to be misunderstood at this point. Scripture's warning against a rosy view of the past is in no way to be read as an absolute ban on the comparison of past with present. Indeed, in the history of the church and in the lives of individuals, some periods have been better than others, and these are things we most certainly do need to know about. Why, then, is God warning us against a rosy view of the past?

First, it is the essential characteristic of the unbeliever. The person with no future hope can only look back. Second, it frequently becomes a substitute for action. We complain about the present, and do nothing ourselves. Third, it is a discouragement to other believers. Constant unfavourable comparisons of the present with the past are often, at root, an implied criticism of what fellow believers are working and praying for *now*. It is no help to a Sunday school teacher or a young people's leader to be repeatedly told that many more children were attending the meetings at such and such a time in the past. Fourth, it is very often misguided. It underestimates the evils of earlier days and ignores the blessings of the present. This was precisely the sin of the children of Israel on their return from captivity. They were despising the day of small things (Zech. 4:10). Recollections of numbers attending meetings in the past are liable to exaggeration. More seriously, numbers are a poor yardstick of the worth of any activity. Most older people can recall times when churches were fuller than today. What they may not realize is the extent to which such religious observance was merely a form of social respectability, which served at its worst to reinforce ill-founded spiritual complacency. The biblical position is nearer to Matthew Henry's reminder that 'God has always been good, and men have always been bad'.

Finally, nostalgia may be a symptom of unbelief. At the laying of the foundation of the second temple, after the return of the Jews from captivity, the people shouted with praise and joy to the Lord —that is, all except the older generation of priests and heads of families. These remembered the glory of the first temple, and they wept aloud. Haggai put his finger on the problem. They were not to be driven into inaction by their nostalgia. '"Be strong . . . and work. For I am with you," declares the Lord Almighty. "This is what I covenanted with you when you came out of Egypt. And my Spirit remains among you. Do not fear' (Hag. 2:4-5; cf. Ezra 3:11-12). In their regrets at the small scale of the temple, they were in danger of making a practical denial of the presence of God.

Our attitude should be rather that of the psalmist, in the 'psalm of old age' (Ps.71). Conscious of his weakness, and anxious that he is unfit for God's service, he is none the less concerned for the prosperity of future generations. There is much to be done, and he is eager to do it. As with Jacob on his deathbed, we may look back to God's saving dealings with us, and forward with the confidence of God's continuing presence with His people (Gen. 48:3,21).

Pride

One of the difficulties faced by Job in his affliction was that the advice which his experience and conscience rejected came from men who had been longer in the field than himself. Indeed, his friends were not slow to remind him of this. 'What do you know that we do not know? What insights do you have that we do not have? The grey-haired and the aged are on our side, men even older than your father' (Job 15:9-10). Age and experience, they assumed, brought wisdom, and they were proud of that fact. But they were wrong. Indeed, whatever *ought* to be the case, all too often the old seem unable to give the advice and spiritual wisdom that is needed, so that we may even go as far as Job in his complaint that God 'takes away the understanding of the aged' (Job 12:20 AV). Later in the same book, Elihu is right to give deference to years, and allow his friends to answer Job first; but he is right also to conclude that men of great age are not necessarily men of great wisdom (Job 32:6-9). Grey hair is a crown of splendour, but only when it is attained by a righteous life (Prov. 16:31).

With increasing age we may find ourselves more able to view with tolerance the excesses and mistakes of others. This is a two-sided coin, however, and though we may have been among the most zealous and orthodox in our youth, there is no guarantee that we will not grow to treasure a sinful peace. This can show itself in a constant, unquestioning deprecation of the zeal of young believers, and an unteachable spirit. 'Better a poor but wise youth than an old but foolish king who no longer knows how to take warning', is Scripture's answer (Eccles. 4:13).

Loss of spiritual vigour

We are in danger of behaving as if older Christians are somehow immune to the temptations and spiritual ups and downs that affect ourselves. Yet old age may itself be a time of backsliding. It was as Solomon grew old that his wives turned his heart after other gods.

Falling away may be a sudden event. However, it is the gradual loss of spiritual vigour that we need particularly to guard against in old age. In the same way that colour rinses can hide our grey hairs, so can we conceal and blind ourselves to the gradual increase of spiritual greyness (Hos. 7:9). The end result of this path is the state of the church at Sardis, which had a reputation of being alive but was dead (Rev. 3:1).

This condition is, by definition, resistant to recovery. Have I experienced such spiritual decay? At least, do I have a sense of my proneness to it? If not, it is likely either that I have never known a spiritually flourishing state, or that I am spiritually asleep (Rev.

3:17). Have I been able, in recent months, to maintain a spiritual peace and joy in my soul? If not, what is the reason? Have I become weary in well doing, indeed, weary of God Himself? Do I murmur with the people of Malachi's day, 'What a burden!', and in so doing run the awful risk of making God weary with me (Mal. 1:13; 2:17; Isa. 1:13-14)? Are my spiritual graces 'fresh and green', or have I lost my appetite for the food of my soul (Ps. 92:14; 1 Pet. 2:2-3)? I am hearing the Word preached as much as ever, but am I hearing it with the same desire and spiritual relish as before? Have I become so full of the things of this life that I 'loathe honey' (Prov. 27:7)?

SPIRITUAL EXPECTATIONS OF OLD AGE

An all-important assumption must be brought out before we consider the particular spiritual hallmarks that ought to characterize the elderly believer. It is in the very nature of spiritual life to grow, and the elderly Christian is not exempt. We may reach physical old age, but we must never reach spiritual old age. When the Bible talks about spiritual maturity, the metaphor used is not that of old age, but of adulthood. We are to heed the observation of the Puritan Thomas Taylor that 'God's school is for old men as well as young', and 'every man must labour to recompense the decay of nature with increase of grace'.

Do not misunderstand the remarks. There are spiritual graces appropriate to a particular time of life. Failing eyesight may prevent us reading substantial Christian books—that is the work of younger eyes. But our path is to be 'like the first gleam of dawn, shining ever brighter till the full light of day' (Prov. 4:18). How can we be certain that we will not lose a sense of peace, joy and comfort should afflictions and troubles gather round us? Though outwardly wasting away, Paul did not lose heart. Why? Because inwardly he was being renewed day by day. Both in weight and duration the unseen glory to which he looked far surpassed his present troubles (2 Cor. 4:16-18).

Growth in grace not only provides a cast-iron source of comfort to the believer, it also glorifies Christ. The righteous 'will still bear fruit in old age, they will stay fresh and green, proclaiming, "The Lord is upright; he is my Rock, and there is no wickedness in him"' (Ps. 92:14-15). Let us emulate Andrew Bonar, who, on his seventy-ninth birthday, spent the whole morning offering the remarkable prayer 'that my latter days may be days of rapid progress in the knowledge of Christ'.

Long experience of God's ways should bring with it certain

characteristics. David's long knowledge of God gave him a sense of assurance. He could look back over his life and conclude, 'I was young and now I am old, yet I have never seen the righteous forsaken or their children begging bread' (Ps. 37:25). This assurance should yield patience. Older men, says Paul to Titus, are to be 'sound . . . in endurance' (Titus 2:2), that is, patient. Doubtless, part of the reason for this exhortation is that old people, perhaps especially men, may grow touchy and impatient. Yet there are, as we have just observed, positive reasons for enduring. In one of his last letters, the late Rev. Kenneth McCrae wrote, 'I believe that I can set my teeth and hold on, but that is all I am good for.' May God give us older believers who have that virtue! Thomas Taylor suggests five characteristics of patience, which ought to hold good for the elderly believer: to entertain all crosses alike, to be cheerful in affliction, to be thankful in affliction, to expect God's deliverance and to resign one's self totally to the will of God. The older believer should be characterized by a spiritual far-sightedness. It took years of hard training under God's hand, but by his old age Jacob had gained such qualities. Can it be said of those of us who are old that we are people of spiritual strength and sound judgment?

Old age brings a lessening of activity and a slower pace of life. Christians ought to take advantage of this opportunity and use it to the maximum. Without the demands of being in a place of work by a certain hour in the morning, the believer can more easily set apart a convenient time of each day for sustained prayer for fellow believers. A widow left all alone, says Paul, may spend day and night in prayer, and while he is particularly talking of seeking the help of God for one's own needs (1 Tim. 5:5), the same principle applies to intercessory prayer on behalf of others. The older believer should never feel that, in the work of the church, there is nothing left for him or her to do. Moreover, prayer 'cancels loneliness' (Oswald Sanders). It deepens fellowship with God and embraces a wide circle of people. But we are to be warned that we cannot expect to relish spiritual privileges in old age if we have not learned their preciousness in younger years.

Concern for the unbeliever should not stop with prayer, however. The older Christian is to do his utmost to win others for the Saviour. It is to be feared that some of the older Christians in our congregations would be afflicted almost with horror at the thought of speaking openly to someone about the Lord Jesus Christ. Yet why not? You have the time to engage in conversation. Many of you have the physical health and enough of this world's goods to be able to offer hospitality. Furthermore, you are in an ideal position to witness to others. Younger Christians sometimes find it hard to speak plainly to people older than themselves. You do not have this disadvantage. Be plain, be gracious, be simple, be urgent and bold, as God gives you opportunity. You more than anyone know how fleeting time is.

Finally, old age for the Christian is perhaps inevitably a time of mixed feelings: a sense of assurance, yet a deep awareness of one's own failings; a desire to be gone, and yet a realization of all that still remains to be done. This godly dissatisfaction was evident in the apostle as he neared his end. He was ready to depart, having fought the good fight and finished the race. He had no bitter self-recrimination, despite his consciousness of being the chief of sinners. Yet in almost the same breath he is warning Timothy of all that still lies ahead, with its temptations, difficulties and opportunities (2 Tim. 4:1-8). Likewise with Joshua and his closest spiritual companion Caleb. Joshua was old and well advanced in years when 'the Lord said to him, "You are very old, and there are still very large areas of land to be taken over".' Caleb was 85, and for 45 years he had nourished in his heart the promise that God would bring him into possession of that land which, in his whole-hearted trust in God, he had been ready to enter after his first spying visit. 'Now give me this hill country that the Lord promised me that day', he asked Joshua (Josh. 13:1; 14:12). May God grant to His church 85-year-olds like Caleb who, however frail their physical frame, have put on the full armour of God, so that when the day of evil comes they are able to stand their ground, and after they have done everything, stand. These will be they who, when they come to die, will have nothing to do but die.

THE ELDERLY AND OURSELVES

Much of what has been said so far has been directed at the elderly person, and particularly the Christian. Yet those who are 65 or older only account for 15 per cent of our population. What about the attitudes and responsibilities of the rest of us?

Before launching into practical prescriptions, we need to assimilate the general guiding principles provided in Scripture. Otherwise, our practical efforts will prove only a prop to the creaking apparatus of the Welfare State.

Attitudes to the elderly

One of the most appalling aspects of the present age is the decline in attitudes and behaviour towards the old. I can still remember, with shock, hearing of a boy I had known who had assaulted and killed an old lady in her own home after she apparently refused to give him her money. Such examples are, fortunately, still very rare. Furthermore, we should be careful before we jump to a rash or simple conclusion about who or what is to blame for this malaise.

None the less, the contrast between the simple biblical principles and daily experience is evident. Love and respect are the twin precepts of God's Word. Love, because of the pattern of Christ's love for us. Christ's love involved self-denial to people far below Him, who could offer no recompense, and even when they were opposed to Him (2 Cor. 8:9). Our concern for cantankerous old people should exhibit the same qualities. Moreover, it is love in Christ. So Paul could appeal to Philemon for Onesimus, 'as Paul—an old man'. 'I appeal to you on the basis of love', he wrote; that is, the love in Christ which he knew Philemon to have demonstrated to the saints (Philem. 7-9).

If we are to show love because of what we know to be true of God's grace in the gospel, then the same is true of the requirement that we show respect. The injunction to Moses brings this out clearly. 'Rise in the presence of the aged, show respect for the elderly and revere your God. I am the Lord' (Lev. 19:32). If Lot had displayed respect to his elderly uncle Abraham, he would never have found himself in Sodom. In the New Testament Timothy is counselled to treat an older man as if he were his father, and an older woman as if she were his mother (1 Tim. 5:1,2). Yet the context of this advice should not escape us. Paul is telling Timothy how he should deal with correcting the elderly in his congregation. Too frequently we fail to observe the proper balance. While we are to show respect, we are culpable in the extreme if we simply ignore the failings of the elderly. This is to fall into Confucius' mistake, who taught that, 'When you are seventy you can follow the devices and desires of your heart without sin'! Rather, says Paul, we are to deal with them in a positive fashion—by exhorting, rather than by rebuking harshly. As Hendriksen remarks, perhaps with slight wryness, 'to correct one's own mother surely requires deep humility, genuine searching of heart, wrestling at the throne of grace, wisdom'.

This emphasis highlights one reason why, in God's eyes, the old may not gain respect—because they have not earned and do not deserve it. Paul tells Titus to teach the older men to be worthy of respect, and older women not to be slanderers, and the apostle was not in the habit of warning against non-existent hazards. One reason why we should not be too quick to blame only the younger generation for the problems of our day may lie in the fact that not all old people are worthy of respect.

102

Some practical suggestions

The twin requirements of love and respect, each presented with a distinctively Christian motive, need to be worked out thoroughly in a practical way. Christians have already made a mark in this area. A recent research study of patterns of informal neighbourhood care revealed that those people who volunteered for altruistic reasons were often largely church-based. Furthermore, these were the very people who could be relied on to undertake long-term support in the more demanding situations.

Recent government policies in this country have weakened the Welfare State, and placed more emphasis on informal care in the community. Whatever we may think of such policies, Christians ought to be in the forefront—demonstrating our love of truth by truthful love, as Spurgeon remarked in a similar context.

In applying this concern to the elderly, we are left with ample room for manoeuvre. A simple comparison of a geriatric ward with conditions in most children's hospitals gives evidence of the frequent indifference with which the old are treated. The concluding suggestions are in no way exhaustive. They are simply selected from a range of possible examples.

Retirement is not the creation of the modern State. Scripture gives clear guidance (e.g. Num. 8:23-26; Lev. 27:7; 1 Tim. 5). In the Old Testament, retirement ages were laid down for Levites. After retirement at the age of 50 they were not to be left idle. At their own discretion they could continue to care for the tabernacle. It is equally unwise in our own day for the elderly to be suddenly cut off from all useful labour. Many Christians belong to independent churches. For them, there are particular matters related to the retirement of the minister. We need to ensure that some adequate pension provision is made. We cannot regret the fact that the minister's wife works if we are falling down in our practical support of the ministry.

The tied house is another tradition which many evangelical churches have inherited from the past. In days of limited geographical mobility, the lack of security created for ministers living in tied houses was less evident. It seems difficult to justify its continuance today.

Housing affects other people in the congregation, in addition to the minister. The Aged Pilgrims' Friend Society has made an important contribution to the housing needs of elderly believers. More remains to be done. Some churches have already taken practical steps, through the setting up of housing associations, and more co-operation is needed in this sphere. On a less ambitious level, individual churches may be in a position to set aside particular properties for the use of elderly people in their congregation. Local authority Social Services Departments may be willing to install aids and adaptations. At the very least, they ought to provide advice on the kind of adaptations needed.

Some problems are less tangible than housing. Many elderly people would value the company of fellow Christians or of young people. With the minimum of organization, a young people's meeting could take on responsibilities of this kind.

Stuart Olyott discusses the opportunities for fostering children elsewhere in this book. The increase in numbers of elderly people has prompted the consideration of fostering schemes for the elderly. Quite clearly, there are considerable implications for families who are willing to help in this way. However, its thoughtful consideration by Christians is to be recommended. Your own local authority may be able to give you advice. In addition, local churches may have families within their membership who could take an elderly Christian into their home. With careful planning, it may be possible for the church to provide financial support in such cases. One church in Wales has undertaken the partial support of a Christian woman in the fellowship, who is working among elderly people in the congregation.

The emphasis in this final section has deliberately focused on the practical and social needs of the elderly. There is much to be said in support of the argument that the spiritual needs of the elderly should be met within the normal pattern of church fellowship and evangelism.

> There is no such thing as a special gospel for the young, and a special gospel for the middle-aged, and a special gospel for the aged. There is only one gospel, and we must always be careful not to tamper and tinker with the gospel as a result of recognizing these age distinctions. At the same time, there is a difference in applying this one and only gospel to the different age groups.
>
> D. M. Lloyd-Jones

Here I would enter a plea for the consideration of formal and informal house meetings for the elderly, with a clear evangelistic purpose. Elderly Christians have an ideal opportunity to open their homes to their neighbours and in this way provide an outlet for the prayer and witness referred to earlier.

Other practical suggestions need to be worked out. But whatever we do, may we be able to echo Philip Doddridge's words:

> *His work my hoary age shall bless,*
> *When youthful vigour is no more;*
> *And my last hour of life confess*
> *His love hath animating power.*

FURTHER READING

J. Oswald Sanders—*Enjoying Growing Old* (Kingsway, 1981). This practical and biblical book is to be recommended. He applies a wide range of biblical principles to many aspects of growing old. There is a short but helpful article by John Marsh, 'On the Subject of Growing Old', in the *Christian Graduate* of December 1978. He writes in epistolary style, as did Archibald Alexander in his excellent series of 'Letters to the Aged', printed in his *Thoughts on Religious Experience* (Banner of Truth, 1967). John Newton also deals with the question in his three letters on growth in grace (*Letters*, Banner of Truth 1960). John Owen's application of the theme of spiritual backsliding to old believers is particularly provoking (*Works*, Vol. 1, Banner of Truth, 1965, pp.432-461) and if you can get hold of it, there is a priceless exhortation to the elderly by Philip Henry reprinted in the April 1969 *Banner of Truth* magazine. Finally, perhaps the most helpful all-round book to put into the hands of older Christians is Cornelis Gilhuis, *Conversations on Growing Older* (Eerdmans, 1977). This book has the added attraction of being printed in a larger than usual type size.

8

Divorce

NEIL C. RICHARDS

Inasmuch as what follows is an exposition of the law of God it is applicable to all men. But it has been written with a particular class of people in view—those who have believed on Jesus Christ for salvation and who, out of love and gratitude, wish to walk in the light of His Word. The moral law is not a means of salvation (the law was never given to that end), but a guide and a teacher to those whose sins have already been freely pardoned through the merits of Christ's death.

Some of the reasons for considering this subject can be stated as follows:

1. The whole concept of marriage is being challenged in our day, not only by young people who prefer to live together without taking vows in case things do not work out, but also by sociologists who advance more sophisticated reasons for abandoning the Christian concept of marriage.

2. This spirit of change is reflected in the introduction of the new divorce law. The Reform Bill of 1969 which became law in 1971 made sweeping changes. All grounds for divorce have been reduced to one—'the irretrievable breakdown of the marriage'. The term 'divorce' is no longer used; the marriage is simply said to be dissolved. The law makes no attempt to distinguish between the innocent and the guilty partner; it is no part of the court's task to apportion blame.

3. The figures given in the Introduction to this book show the enormous increase in the divorce rate. In 1968 the figure was about 55,000. The 1971 divorce reform legislation followed, and the latest figures stand at 150,000. The numbers of divorce petitions filed are even higher. On some estimates, one in three marriages contracted this year will end in divorce. The rate of divorce in the case of second marriages is higher still.

No government survey can ever measure the pain and bitterness caused, or the appalling effects on the children, torn between the mother who usually has the care of them and the father who has access to them. Furthermore, there is the problem of maintenance. Half of all the maintenance orders are in arrears. The suicide rate among divorcees is six times higher than the national average. All this has led to a demand for further reform of the divorce law. Nowhere are the tragic effects of humanism and atheism seen more starkly than here in the break-up of family life.

4. Evangelical churches are by no means immune to the effects of this moral downgrade. Pastors and elders are confronted in their churches by complex and painful marital problems which were hardly known 30 years ago.

5. Although some progress has been made by evangelicals in recent years towards a more united testimony and practice in this area, a measure of confusion still remains. The result is that the decision of one church can be overturned by another.

6. Even where there is clarity on the main principles of Scripture governing divorce, the work of applying these principles to particular cases can be very difficult and often gives rise to acute pastoral problems.

THE HISTORICAL ASPECT

In its statement on marriage and divorce, the Westminster Confession of 1646 allows for divorce and remarriage on the grounds of adultery, and also on the grounds of wilful desertion by the unbelieving partner.[1] It would seem that this represents the prevailing view in the seventeenth century, although for some reason all reference to divorce is omitted from the Savoy Declaration of 1658 and the Baptist Confession of 1689. However, so far as the law of the land is concerned, until the middle of the nineteenth century a special Act of Parliament was necessary before a man could obtain a legal divorce. In 1857 the Matrimonial Clauses Act allowed full divorce in cases of adultery; and in 1937 the Herbert Act extended the grounds of divorce to include desertion, cruelty and incurable insanity.

Whilst the State was gradually opening the door to divorce, the Anglican Church was rapidly closing it. By the end of the nineteenth century the view that marriage is indissoluble and that divorce does not give the right to remarriage had become widely held, and all second marriages of those whose partners were still living were forbidden. Several factors contributed to this change: firstly, the rise of New Testament criticism, and the subsequent questioning of the validity of the exceptive clause in Matthew as an authentic word of Christ; secondly, the rise of the Anglo-Catholic movement, with its moral theology largely derived from the Roman Church; and, thirdly, the fact that divorce was no longer an exceptional occurrence, but came to be viewed as a major challenge to the Christian view of marriage.[2]

These trends in Anglican thinking and practice influenced the Free Churches, so that today evangelicals are often 'Anglican' in their views of divorce—allowing separation but not remarriage.[3]

THE TEACHING OF CHRIST

In seeking to establish our Lord's teaching on this matter, we shall examine two key passages in Matthew's Gospel.

Matthew 5:31-32

These words are found in what is usually known as the Sermon on the Mount, and in that section of the discourse where our Lord is unfolding the true meaning of the law of God and refuting the false interpretation of the Pharisees. We can consider the teaching of these verses under three headings:

a) *The Old Testament teaching on divorce*

The main passage of Scripture to be considered in this connection is Deuteronomy 24:1-4. (A full exegesis is provided by Professor John Murray in his book *Divorce*.) We can summarize it by stating that the whole purpose of the Mosaic legislation was to curb sin. Men were putting away their wives for the most trivial reasons, and the result was great hardship, suffering and misery, both for wives and children. The legislation was designed to restrain this sin. Divorce was tolerated and suffered by God, but it did not have the divine sanction and was no part of His original purpose.

The legislation curbed sin in three ways. In the first place, it restricted the grounds of divorce to more serious offences; secondly, it insisted that a legal bill of divorce be given; and, thirdly, it forbade husbands to remarry their divorced wives.

With respect to the restriction as to the grounds of divorce, the question which arises is, What is this 'uncleanness' of which Moses speaks? It is clearly not adultery. The law of Moses prescribed death for that offence (Lev. 20:10; Deut. 22:22). It was evidently some behaviour which was shameful and offensive, though it is difficult to determine its precise nature. What we can affirm, however, is that the legislation excluded reasons that were slight and trivial.

109

b) *The teaching of the scribes and Pharisees*

The scribes and Pharisees turned this toleration and sufferance on God's part into a precept and a directive. They taught that men ought to put away their wives even for the most trivial cause. This abuse of the law caused a great deal of suffering and misery.

c) *Our Lord's teaching*

In contradistinction to this our Lord said: 'But I say unto you, that whosoever shall put away his wife, saving for the cause of fornication, causeth her to commit adultery: and whosoever shall marry her that is divorced committeth adultery' (Matt. 5:32). Thus He brings to an end the Old Testament law which required the death penalty for adultery, abrogates all other Mosaic legislation regarding divorce, and in its place makes adultery the sole ground for divorce.[4]

The word translated 'fornication' (*porneia*) is a generic term for all sexual immorality and included every kind of unlawful sexual intercourse. Outside of marriage it means fornication: within marriage it means adultery.[5] The fact that this exceptive clause occurs only in Matthew in no way casts doubt upon its authenticity; neither is there any textual evidence for questioning the genuineness of the clause.

Adultery is the sole ground for divorce because only adultery violates the marriage bond. Christ forbids a man to 'put away' his wife for any other reason. If he does so, he causes her to commit adultery—that is, he puts her in a position in which she is tempted to join herself to another man and thereby commit adultery. Whoever marries her also commits adultery. Why is this? It can only be that where divorce is illegitimate, the marriage bond is still existent. The two are still in reality and before God bound to one another in matrimony.

Matthew 19:3-9

Our Lord is confronted here by a direct question, 'Is it lawful for a man to put away his wife for every cause?' He replies by stating the original purpose of marriage: 'For this cause shall a man leave father and mother, and shall cleave to his wife: and they twain shall be one flesh . . . What therefore God hath joined together, let not man put asunder.' The Pharisees, failing in their attempt to catch Jesus out, put a further question: 'Why did Moses then command to give a writing of divorcement, and to put her away?' Jesus gave a twofold reply:

a) This legislation was introduced because of 'the hardness of your hearts'—that is, because of your sin and perversity. (We have already commented upon this.)

b) Such divorce legislation was not a part of God's original purpose for marriage: 'but from the beginning it was not so'. God suffered this state of things for a while, but it was not in line with His original design.[6]

So we come to verse 9, perhaps the most important verse in the Gospels on this matter. It brings together two clauses—the exceptive clause ('except it be for fornication') and the remarriage clause ('and shall marry another'). Both these clauses occur elsewhere, but only here are they co-ordinated.

The question which arises is, May the innocent party remarry? On this question the professing church is sharply divided. There are those who maintain that adultery gives grounds for separation from bed and board, but does not sever the marriage bond and so does not give the right to divorce and remarriage. This is the avowed position of the Roman Catholic Church, though she does have ways of getting round it by saying that not *all* marriages are true marriages. As David Field puts it, 'So a Roman Catholic divorcee who seeks remarriage will find the church door securely locked and bolted against him; but on it, if he looks carefully, he may see a small notice which says "Please come round the back".' [7] It is also the position of the Anglican Church (except that it has no back door), and of many evangelical Free Churchmen, who will allow separation, and even divorce, but not remarriage.

The correct exegesis of this text is, therefore, all-important. At this point the commentaries are disappointing. Even William Hendriksen's fine volume contains only the most general treatment of this text. John Murray gives a detailed exegesis, to which we are indebted, and Jay Adams also provides a helpful treatment (in *Marriage, Divorce and Remarriage*).

The chief exegetical question is, Does the exceptive clause apply both to the 'putting away' and to the remarriage? There is strong ground for asserting that it does. The subject dealt with in the text is 'putting away' and remarriage; the two cannot be separated, and it would be wrong to relate the exceptive clause to anything less than both co-ordinates. Just as whoever divorces his wife on the grounds of adultery *does not sin*, so whoever divorces his wife on these grounds and marries another *does not sin*. The exceptive clause applies to both divorce and remarriage.

It is an interesting fact that scholars like Charles Gore, who was so influential at the beginning of the century in bringing the Church of England to a position of denying the right of remarriage, recognized that the exceptive clause applied to remarriage as well as to 'putting away'. He got round this by regarding the exceptive clause as a later interpolation and not an authentic word of Christ.

Furthermore, if adultery 'rises in rebellion against the very essence of the marriage bond',[8] and divorce dissolves that bond, it is difficult to see upon what grounds the innocent party can be forbidden to remarry.

In the light of our Lord's teaching it is difficult to see why David Field, in his otherwise helpful treatment of the subject, should expect the Christian to sympathize with the terms of the divorce legislation under which a single act of adultery may not constitute grounds for divorce, and where all reference to guilty and innocent partners is excluded.[9] If we are to take our Lord's teaching seriously, judgments have to be made between guilt and innocence, however difficult that may be at times. Where there is no adultery, there is no ground for divorce.

One final word must be added. Our Lord is not here *commanding* divorce in the case of adultery. Wherever possible, mercy and love and forgiveness should operate. The believer, having received such forgiveness and grace from God, must always be poised in readiness to forgive others. There is no justification here for a hard and legal attitude which demands its rights and is void of pity.

THE TEACHING OF PAUL

The key passage for consideration here is 1 Corinthians 7:10-15. In the opening verses of the section (10,11) Paul is not dealing with divorce but with separation, and the problems which he has in view do not involve adultery. He begins by forbidding separation: 'Let not the wife depart from her husband.' Every endeavour is to be made to maintain the marriage; but if separation does occur, 'let her remain unmarried'.

Paul is here dealing with marriage where both partners are believers. He does not condone separation, but simply recognizes the perversity of human nature, even in believers, and says, 'If separation occurs, then you must seek reconciliation; but, failing that, no other marriage relationship is to be entered into.' This passage has often been regarded as supporting the legitimacy of separation without remarriage when the strains within the marriage have become overwhelming, but it is doubtful whether Paul is really saying as much as that. John Murray is probably right when he says that Paul is simply dealing with a situation that had actually arisen in the church.[10]

The apostle turns to a different situation in verse 12. Here one partner is a believer and the other is not. 'But to the rest speak I, not the Lord.' Clearly Paul is not drawing a distinction between inspired and authoritative statements on the one hand and his own ministerial judgment on the other. That would be contrary to the whole tone of verse 17: 'And so ordain I in all churches.' There is no reduction in authority. He is simply drawing a distinction between what Christ taught during the days of His earthly ministry and his own apostolic authority. In verses 10 and 11 he could refer directly to our Lord's teaching when on earth, but now he is moving into a situation with which Jesus did not deal. As John Stott puts it, 'His contrast is not between what is divine and infallible and what is human and fallible, but between two forms of divine, infallible instruction, the one dominical and the other apostolic.' [11]

The verse which especially concerns us is verse 15: 'But if the unbelieving depart, let him depart. A brother or a sister is not under bondage in such cases: but God hath called us to peace.' The unbelieving partner has deserted—a situation not uncommon in a debased and immoral city like Corinth. What then should the believing partner do? Paul's ruling is that though the believer must *never* take the initiative in such a move, or give any encouragement to the unbelieving partner to desert, yet, if the separation does take place, it should be allowed to take its course. 'A brother or a sister is not under bondage in such cases.'

The crucial question is, What does Paul mean by the term 'is not bound'? Does he simply mean that the believing partner is no longer under obligation to discharge marital duties towards the deserting spouse? It cannot mean less than that, and there is good evidence to show that it means more. According to the more limited meaning (see Appendix), Paul is teaching that the believing partner is not to be troubled in conscience by the enforced state of separation, but is to be comforted by the knowledge that he or she is no longer encumbered by the duties and preoccupations of married life (vv.32-35). The 'bondage', by this view, is not the marriage bond itself, but the restrictions of married life which prevent men attending as they might upon the things of the Lord. The words 'but God hath called us to peace' are then taken as a call to seek peace and understanding in the marriage, and verse 16 ('For what knowest thou, O wife, whether thou shalt save thy husband . . .?') as an added incentive to maintain the marriage bond and certainly not to seek a divorce. Our Lord's teaching on the one exceptive case of adultery is regarded as giving further support to this interpretation.

113

There are other considerations, however, which favour a stronger meaning, namely, that such wilful desertion is ground for divorce and so for remarriage:

a) The word used for separation (*chōrizō*—'depart') was often used as a synonym for the verb 'to divorce'.[12]

b) The Greek verb in the phrase 'is not bound' is in the perfect tense, indicating a permanent state of freedom.

c) In verses 27 and 39, and in Romans 7:2, Paul speaks of the bond of marriage and uses the verb *deō* (for example, 'the wife is bound as long as her husband liveth'). If this verb has reference to the bond of marriage, then its negative form would indicate freedom from such a bond. The verb used in verse 15, however, is *douloō*, and this is a stronger word than *deō*. In Acts 7:6 it refers to Israel's bondage in Egypt, and in 2 Peter 2:19 it is used of bondage to sin. So, considering both this and the context of *ou dedoulōtai* ('is not bound'), there are good grounds for taking it to mean freedom from the marriage bond.[13]

d) The words, 'but God hath called us to peace', probably refer to the whole treatment of mixed marriages, and not simply to the last clause. The gospel is not designed to break up families, and so the believer should do all that he can to prevent disruption; but if it comes, he is not to expose himself to strife and frustration; rather, he is to allow the separation to take its course. The interpretation of these words depends largely upon the interpretation of the former part of the verse, and the same can be said for verse 16. If the stronger interpretation of verse 15 is accepted, then in verse 16 Paul is saying that marriage is not to be regarded simply as an evangelistic opportunity. To cling to a marriage which the unconverted partner has determined to end leads only to frustration and tension.[14]

But how can we reconcile this interpretation with our Lord's teaching on the one exceptive case of adultery?

1. Our Lord is dealing with the question of 'putting away': Paul is dealing with wilful desertion.

2. Paul is obviously dealing in verses 12 ff. with cases which do not come within the orbit of Christ's teaching. 'But to the rest say I, not the Lord.'

3. It is a feasible assumption that our Lord was dealing with cases in which both partners are believers by profession. This assumption is confirmed by what Paul says in verses 10 and 11: there he is dealing

114

with cases in which both partners are believers, and there he appeals to the teaching of our Lord.

4. Paul's language is very different in the two cases. In the first (vv. 10,11) he exhorts to reconciliation and warns against any thought of entry into another marriage. In the second (v.15) he speaks quite differently: 'But if the unbelieving depart, let him depart,' and then he says that the deserted partner 'is not bound'. They are two very different cases. Our Lord does not deal with the second case.

One further point must be added. We must note carefully the limited circumstances to which the words of the apostle Paul relate:

(i)   He is dealing with mixed marriages, and not with marriages between two believers or two unbelievers.

(ii)   The case in view is one of wilful desertion by the unbelieving partner. The believer is never to take the initiative or to give any encouragement.

(iii)   The separation must be conceived as finding its roots in a basic difference arising from the believer's profession and practice of the Christian faith.

Summary

1. God's original intention in ordaining marriage was that it should be a permanent and exclusive union between one man and one woman. Only within this marriage union may sexual desires be satisfied and procreation take place.

2. The marriage bond is radically disrupted only in two cases: first, in the case of adultery, and, secondly, in the case of wilful desertion by the unbelieving partner. In neither case is divorce commanded; it should only be resorted to when all else has failed. Such divorce leaves the innocent partner free to remarry.

PRACTICAL APPLICATION

It is as we enter the field of pastoral responsibility and church discipline that we are confronted by very considerable difficulties.[15] We have no desire to be legalistic, but we have to make spiritual and moral judgments in this realm. For the Christian who has problems in this area and whose conscience is sensitive to the Word and the Spirit, it is of the greatest importance that he or she knows what is right and what is wrong.

Reference must be made at this point to the view that when a man becomes a Christian he has a 'fresh start', and past marital problems involving divorce can be forgotten. Just as the apostle

Paul viewed his persecuting activity against the church as being done 'ignorantly in unbelief' (1 Tim. 1:13), so, according to this view, those divorced on unscriptural grounds before their conversion acted in ignorance and are not required to take the past into account when contemplating future marriage arrangements. Thus a man who before his conversion divorced his wife because their marriage had become stale and loveless would, on becoming a Christian, be perfectly free to remarry.

Is this, however, a legitimate inference from Paul's words? Surely the point Paul is making is that, although his past conduct had been so fearfully wicked, yet it had not been wilful sin against the light, such as the Scripture speaks of in Matthew 12:31-32, Hebrews 6:4-6, Hebrews 10:26 and 1 John 5:16. Paul is not lessening the enormity of his guilt, for his ignorance was culpable; but it was still not of such a kind as to put him beyond the pale of mercy. To argue that Paul's involvement in the death of Stephen made him guilty of murder and liable to punishment by the civil law, but that conversion gave him a 'fresh start', is to go well beyond the facts of Scripture. Doubtless Paul was guilty of a breach of the sixth commandment, but he acted, as did others, in obedience (as they thought) to the Old Testament law which required the death of blasphemers.

The biblical teaching on sins committed before conversion is surely this: they are fully and freely pardoned through the merits of Christ's blood, but the earthly consequences of these sins often remain and must be suffered. For example, the thief must restore what he has stolen and suffer the punishment due to his crimes; the debtor must pay his debts, and the man divorced from his wife for no proper reason must not enter into a new marriage relationship even after conversion.

Now the problem is a complex one. What if his former wife remarries? We might arrive at the conclusion that the Christian is then free to remarry. Certainly there are marital situations that cannot be put right, and clearly in such cases the believer is not to be burdened in his conscience.

1. What should be our attitude towards the State laws on divorce?

Should the State allow divorce only on the two grounds allowed in Scripture? or is this expecting too much from a secular State? Can we apply the principle that operated in the Old Testament, that the State should curb marital abuses and sins by allowing divorce for serious breaches of the marriage bond? Is John Stott right in making the following statement?

The State will frame its own divorce laws, and the Church [that is, the Anglican Church] may well have been right to encourage it to adopt the 'irretrievable breakdown' concept as the best and fairest basis for legislation in a secular society. But the Church has its own witness to bear to the teaching of its divine Lord, and must exercise its own discipline.[16]

Is this a possible Christian attitude—that we recognize the limitation of the State in this realm, and concede that she can do little more than restrain the worst abuses, very much as the temporary Mosaic legislation did in the Old Testament; but that as a church we must have different standards and be governed by the teaching of Scripture?

2. Is there a place for ecclesiastical divorce?

Divorce in our modern society falls within the jurisdiction of the civil magistrate. We do not dispute this: marriage deeply concerns the welfare of the community, and so it is within the province of the magistrate to control marriage and its dissolution. But the laws of the State do not coincide with the laws of Scripture, and so the church has her own duty to perform.[17]

Consider the following examples:

Example 1. A woman is divorced by her husband on unscriptural grounds. She is quite innocent: he is irresponsible and faithless. The woman is converted and becomes a member of a church. What is her marital position? In the eyes of the State she is divorced and therefore free to remarry. How is the church to view her?

Surely we have to say that the marital bond is still in existence. Her husband has put her away; if she remarries she commits adultery. That is our Lord's teaching.

But what if, after a while, her husband marries another woman, so that he thereby commits adultery and the woman now possesses scriptural grounds for divorce? In the eyes of the State she is already divorced; what is she to do? Might not the church act here? Being satisfied that adultery has taken place, could it not give the woman a bill of divorce? It can then be seen that the church is not governed by the State laws at this point (as they are contrary to God's law), but by the teaching of Christ her Head.[18]

This is by no means a merely academic issue.

Example 2. A woman (a professing believer) divorces her husband on the ground of cruelty. Adultery is involved, but she is advised to seek divorce on other grounds. Later she becomes a member of a church and wishes to remarry. What is her position, and what is the church's duty in the matter?

Ought not the church to give her a divorce on the legitimate ground of adultery and pronounce her free to remarry? If the church does nothing and the woman remarries, then the church appears to condone divorce on grounds other than adultery and desertion.

SOME CONCLUSIONS

1. This is a tremendously sensitive area and needs to be handled in a spirit of Christian love and compassion.

2. We have to recognize that there are situations which cannot be sorted out on earth; there are marital problems that cannot be undone. Where there is faith and repentance, there is forgiveness in Christ; but the earthly consequences of sin may have to be borne.

3. We can exert little influence on the State in these matters, but we can and ought to give attention to these things in the church.

4. If ministers are silent on these matters, there is no doubt that the standards of the world will become the standards of the Lord's people. What is needed at the present hour is for the true church of Christ to be seen to be a separate and distinctive people.

5. We have an obligation to seek to obtain unanimity in truth and practice among the Lord's people. The present divergence in these matters is confusing to believers and dishonouring to God.

6. If it is a part of the purpose of the ministry of the Word in the church to make the people's consciences sensitive to the mind of Christ, then we cannot leave them without scriptural principles to guide them in this matter.

APPENDIX

An alternative interpretation of 1 Corinthians 7:10-15

It has been argued that this passage teaches the radical disruption of the marriage bond by the wilful desertion of an unbelieving partner in a mixed marriage. In this appendix an alternative interpretation of the passage is advanced.

What Paul is saying in these verses is that believers who have to suffer the indignity and hurt of being abandoned by an unbelieving partner may be comforted by the knowledge that they are no longer to be encumbered by the duties and preoccupations of married life: they are no longer 'under bondage'. In other words, far from asserting that the marriage may therefore be dissolved, the apostle is drawing attention to one consideration (an important one in his estimate) which would at least help to compensate for the loss of an unbelieving partner.

In favour of this view would be the following considerations:

1. Without doubt the apostle's overriding concern in writing this part of his letter to the Christians at Corinth is that they should be 'without carefulness' so that they may, if at all possible, 'attend upon the Lord without distraction' (vv.32,35). In his view marriage will have a limiting effect on a Christian's availability for and application to service for his Lord (see especially verses 8, 26, 27b, 28, 29, 32-35, 40). It would not be surprising, therefore, to find him offering this as an element of comfort to a Christian who, because of his or her faith, had been abandoned by the other partner (if only for a period). They would no longer be under the binding obligations imposed by the marriage bond.

2. This interpretation makes the words that follow much more meaningful. In saying, 'but God hath called us to peace', the apostle is clearly adding a cautionary note: even though a partner may have been abandoned temporarily, a Christian must always work for peace and understanding (rather than resort to the total abandonment of the spouse through divorce). In the following verse Paul gives us his reason for making this observation the most important consideration: 'For what knowest thou, O wife, whether thou shalt save thy husband'—though he depart temporarily—'or how knowest thou, O man, whether thou shalt save thy wife?' This is hardly the language of one who believes that separation on religious grounds is sufficient reason for the annulment of what is otherwise considered an indissoluble bond.

3. When it is conceded that the Lord Jesus Christ in His teachings allowed only one ground for divorce, and referred to that one

ground in terms that were clearly meant to be exclusive of any other ('saving for the cause of fornication'), we need to be on guard against accepting too readily any interpretation of this verse that would make the apostle contradict our Lord's unambiguous statement that the only ground for divorce is fornication.

NOTES

1 *The Westminster Confession of Faith* (1647), ch. XXIV, sections v, vi.

2 *Marriage, Divorce and the Church*—report of a Commission appointed by the Archbishop of Canterbury (SPCK, 1971).

3 ibid.

4 D. M. Lloyd-Jones, *Studies in the Sermon on the Mount* (Inter-Varsity Fellowship, 1959), vol. 1, pp.252-61. There is a whole sermon dealing with these verses.

5 For a helpful study of the word see H. M. Carson, 'Divorce', *Banner of Truth*, 209 (February 1981), pp.20-6.

6 John Murray, *Divorce* (Presbyterian & Reformed, 1961).

7 David Field, *Taking Sides* (Inter-Varsity Press, 1975).

8 William Hendriksen, *The Gospel of Matthew* (Banner of Truth, 1974).

9 D. Field, *Taking Sides*, p.66.

10 J. Murray, *Divorce*, pp.65f.

11 John Stott, *Divorce* (Falcon Press, 1971), p.14.

12 D. Field, *Taking Sides*, p.79.

13 J. Murray, *Divorce*, pp.72f.

14 See Charles Hodge and Leon Morris on 1 Corinthians.

15 Andrew R. Anderson, *Marriage, Divorce and Remarriage—an Address to Pastors* (Fellowship of Independent Evangelical Churches, 1980).

16 J. Stott, *Divorce*, p.17.

17 J. Murray, *Divorce*, pp.106f.

18 ibid, pp.107f.

FURTHER READING

There is a fairly wide selection of literature on divorce. The most thorough treatment is John Murray, *Divorce* (Presbyterian & Reformed, 1961). Jay Adams, *Marriage, Divorce and Remarriage in the Bible* (Presbyterian & Reformed, 1980) is very helpful and thorough, and is perhaps the best all-round book. John Stott's *Divorce* (Falcon, 1971) is clear and useful. A more recent contribution by John Stott can be read in his *Issues Facing Christians Today* (Marshall, Morgan & Scott, 1984), chapter 14.

Andrew Anderson's *Marriage, Divorce and Remarriage*, an address given to the annual assembly of FIEC in 1980, is readable and has a firm pastoral concern. This paper can be obtained from the Fellowship of Independent Evangelical Churches, 3 Church Road, Croydon, Surrey CRO 1SG.

9

Abortion and Family Planning

BRIAN HARRIS

1. Abortion

The 1967 Abortion Act looks as if it is with us to stay. When attempts are made to modify it in any way, massive public responses are guaranteed. For example, in 1975, when the issue was being debated in Parliament, it was estimated that at a Sunday rally in London during October of that year, 50,000 people protested at the state of the Abortion Law in this country. On the same day two women chained themselves to the railings of the Houses of Parliament in protest against the protesters! The following week saw a flood of letters to the BBC radio programme 'PM', and the listener was told that these letters were equally divided between support of and opposition to the present situation in the United Kingdom. One correspondent said, 'Of course abortion kills, but it is better to kill a foetus than to maim the lives of existing children by the arrival of another unwanted baby.' Another correspondent raised the provocative question as to why the term used for an unborn child was 'foetus' and not 'baby'!

At about the same time, various points were raised in the House of Commons concerning the Abortion Act. The Minister for Health and Social Services indicated that, in future, private clinics would not be allowed to terminate pregnancies beyond 20 weeks unless they had special operative facilities. The same afternoon the question was put as to why it was difficult to obtain an abortion in certain areas of the country. The answer given was that it was because of the moral objections of consultants in some areas. Another questioner was assured that no directive had ever been issued by the Department of Health and Social Services discriminating against the appointment of doctors who had ethical objections to abortion as consultants in the National Health Service. However, in an article in *The Times* one Member of Parliament declared that he knew of one such case—a senior registrar who, after an interview for a consultant post (at which he was unsuccessful), was told that his best course would be to emigrate.

Various attempts have been made to modify the Act (usually by the introduction of Private Members' Bills), and there is a groundswell of opinion amongst 'conservative Christendom' which from time to time musters its forces. The 'Call to Humanity' rally organized by the Society for the Protection of Unborn Children, involving Malcolm Muggeridge, Rev. John Stott and the late Dr Francis Schaeffer, is but one example of this. Meeting at Hyde Park in June 1983, the rally was a 'memorial' to the 2,000,000 unborn 'children' involved in terminated pregnancies since the Act was introduced.

These illustrations reveal the confused state of affairs in the country at the moment. In the midst of such confusion a strong, clear statement is necessary. It is hoped that this contribution will go some way towards fulfilling that need. Its primary aim is to be biblical, and medical only in a secondary sense: biblical in setting out some guidelines for behaviour, medical in defining and explaining some practical consequences.

In order to appreciate the problems relating to the question of abortion, an acquaintance with the process leading to the birth of a child is essential. The first stage in the formation of a new human being is the union of male and female cells following sexual intercourse. This is known as fertilization, and may occur several days after intercourse. There is a further interval of four to five days before the fertilized egg cell becomes embedded in the wall of the womb. It is important to remember that already there is present in the normal fertilized egg cell the potential to form a human being, to see it through its threescore years and ten, and to control its features. This should be borne in mind when the reader is told that the egg cell is a 'blob of jelly' of no real significance.

Following implantation in the wall of the womb, cell division soon occurs and eventually a ball of cells is formed; this phase lasts approximately three weeks. From the third to the twelfth week of pregnancy this ball of cells is divided into the various parts of the human body, so that a completely formed 'miniature body' exists by the thirteenth week of pregnancy. While in the mother's womb, the developing baby or foetus grows in size to the fully-formed full-term baby of 40 weeks' gestation. Quickening or foetal movements usually begin at about the twenty-second week of pregnancy.

Reasons for consideration

The subject of abortion fully merits our attention at the present time. Reference has already been made to the unsatisfactory and confused terms in which the question is debated in the country. There are other reasons why it deserves careful consideration:

1. *Its relation to the less vexed problem of family planning.*
Abortion can be defined as the termination of pregnancy up until
the twenty-eighth week. It may be spontaneous or procured.
Family planning is usually seen as the control of conception. The
distinction between the two is very fine and not always apparent
immediately. Two examples will suffice. The first is that some
countries, notably Japan, have used procured abortion as a means
of population control at the rate of 1,500,000 annually.[1] Although
not legally permitted as such in this country, many liberal
abortionists hold this view. The second example concerns the use of
intra-uterine coils—the placing of a coil in the womb as a
contraceptive device. It is now generally believed that the way in
which such a coil operates is to prevent implantation of the already
fertilized egg cell in the wall of the womb.[2] This obviously raises a
problem as far as ethics is concerned—is this really a 'termination
of pregnancy'?

2. *The social climate in which we live has changed dramatically in
recent years.* This is reflected in the terms in which the Abortion
Act became law in 1967.[3] The position now is that, with two
medical sponsors, an abortion may be obtained on the following
grounds:

a) Where there is 'risk to the life of the pregnant woman'.
b) Where there is 'risk of injury to the physical or mental health
   of the woman'.
c) Where there is risk of injury to the physical or mental health
   of the existing child (children) of the family of the pregnant
   woman.
d) Where there is substantial risk that if the child were born it
   would suffer from physical or mental abnormalities so as to
   be seriously handicapped.

A conscience clause is included, which is intended to safeguard the
interests of doctors who may have conscientious objections with
regard to abortion.

3. *Apart from the above considerations, how does one interpret
'the will of God' in a given situation?* For example, there is the
genuinely nightmarish problem for the Christian of what to do
when the mother's life is in grave danger should the pregnancy
continue. Is there in those circumstances such a principle as the
lesser of two evils? Does one intervene, or is there a point at which
the individual submits to 'the will of God' in a kind of fatalistic
way?

BIBLICAL PRINCIPLES

In the light of what we have said, our responsibility becomes clear. It is to establish theological principles to guide us in our behaviour. Just as the Christian's view of marriage should be governed by biblical standards and not influenced by changes in the divorce law, so also his opinion concerning pregnancy should not be moulded by the Abortion Act or by what are regarded as medical reasons for abortion. In other words, we return to our original thesis: theological principles are to be our first consideration, and medical indications *must* be subject to these.

An example will serve to show how the conflict may be understood and resolved. Amniocentesis is the name given to a process in which a little of the fluid which surrounds the developing baby is removed and the sex of the baby determined. If the result of this procedure reveals that the baby carries a sex-linked disease, this would presumably constitute *medical* grounds for termination of pregnancy. However, on *theological* grounds it may be decided that abortion is the wrong course of action, and therefore no termination would occur.

Such a view contrasts sharply with the prevailing outlook in society today. Harley Smyth, in a Christian Medical Fellowship booklet, expresses it as follows:

> It should be made clear from the outset, in words as plain as we can find, that abortion (as we have it today) is not primarily a medical matter. Thus, though I write from the perspective of a surgeon and scientist, the central issues before us are moral rather than medical, and ethical rather than scientific. [4]

The Christian, then, will seek pastoral aid and guidance in a particular situation, and one cannot but be unhappy with the concept that the pastor must accept what doctors say. Of course, the situation does arise occasionally when the pastor will have to accept medical advice, as for example when there is danger to the mother's life. But if 'there are profound medical issues to be thought of', [5] the theological issues to be considered are even more profound.

While the task of drawing out principles from Scripture must be approached with caution, it calls at the same time for no small degree of boldness. In the words of Francis Schaeffer,

> We must say that if evangelicals are to be evangelicals we must not compromise our view of Scripture. There is no use in evangelicalism seeming to get larger and larger if at the same time appreciable parts of evangelicalism are getting soft at that which is the core, namely, the Scriptures . . . The issue is clear: is the Bible true, the truth, and

126

infallible wherever it speaks, including where it touches on history and the cosmos, or is it only in some sense revelational when it touches religious subjects? [6]

In looking at biblical principles, it is wise to note that there is no precise parallel to the modern problem of procured (therapeutic) abortion. The introduction to a recent article by A. Gillespie entitled 'Techniques of Abortion' begins, 'Induced abortion has been part of man's history for as long as it has been recorded.' [7] The writer then proceeds to illustrate this. Often medical writers will quote from the Bible as a source of ancient literature, but in this case there is no quotation because no such reference exists. The Scripture does outline, however, certain principles which must surely regulate the conduct of the twentieth-century believer.

Status of foetus

The discussion of the present subject must revolve around the question, What is the status of the foetus? What is it that is carried in the mother's womb? As we examine the Scriptures, we discover that they attribute a very high status to the foetus. It is regarded as a human life second only in status to that of a human being capable of independent existence.

In the first place, the Bible comments on the marvel of life before birth. Ecclesiastes 11:5 states, 'thou knowest not what is the way of the spirit, nor how the bones do grow in the womb of her that is with child: even so thou knowest not the works of God who maketh all'. Here attention is drawn to the formation, development and growth of the baby while still in the womb; it is to be properly regarded as 'a work of God who maketh all'. In that respect, the foetus and the new-born child are equated.

David the psalmist expresses the same wonder in terms of his own experience. As he contemplates the beginnings of God's work in bringing a child into the world, his feelings are of mingled fear, awe and amazement:

> For thou hast possessed my reins; thou hast covered me in my mother's womb. I will praise thee; for I am fearfully and wonderfully made: marvellous are thy works; and that my soul knoweth right well. My substance was not hid from thee, when I was made in secret, and curiously wrought in the lowest parts of the earth. Thine eyes did see my substance, yet being unperfect; and in thy book all my members were written, which in continuance were fashioned, when as yet there was none of them. How precious also are thy thoughts unto me, O God! how great is the sum of them!   Psalm 139:13-17

Turning to the New Testament, we are confronted with a striking example relevant to the subject. In Luke 1:36-44 we have an account of the visit of Mary to her cousin Elizabeth. The mother of John the Baptist was six months pregnant, and when she heard Mary's greeting 'the babe leaped in her womb'. The fact that what is contained within the womb of Elizabeth is called a 'babe'[8] (Greek *brephos*) which is able to 'leap for joy' exemplifies the biblical concept of attributing a very high status to the foetus.

Secondly, other scriptures refer in an indirect way to life in the womb. For instance, the prophet Jeremiah records the word of the Lord to him in these terms: 'Before I formed thee in the belly I knew thee; and before thou camest forth out of the womb I sanctified thee, and I ordained thee a prophet' (Jer. 1:5). Similarly, when the apostle Paul describes his calling to be an apostle and to preach the gospel, he says, '. . . it pleased God, who separated me from my mother's womb' (Gal. 1:15).

One other passage of Scripture must be examined as being germane to this subject, as well as being the occasion of some controversy. It is found in Exodus 21:22-25, and states that in a dispute involving a pregnant woman the law required that certain principles be put into practice. In the Authorized Version the passage reads as follows:

> If men strive, and hurt a woman with child, so that her fruit depart from her, and yet no mischief follow: he shall be surely punished, according as the woman's husband will lay upon him; and he shall pay as the judges determine. And if any mischief follow, then thou shalt give life for life, eye for eye, tooth for tooth, hand for hand, foot for foot, burning for burning, wound for wound, stripe for stripe.

These verses are similarly translated in the Revised Version of 1881, the American Revised Standard Version and the New English Bible. The impression all these translations give is that, in the case of injury or death to the mother, a like retribution should be exacted; but in the case of injury or death to the foetus retribution should be by financial settlement. The implication is obvious. Injury or death in the case of the unborn child is regarded as less serious than injury or death in the case of the mother.

However, another translation and interpretation is quite possible, and this alternative understanding of the passage is held by such men as John Calvin,[9] the commentators Keil and Delitzsch[10] and the Jewish commentator Cassuto.[11] It has been expressed in semi-popular form by J. W. Cotrell in an article entitled 'Abortion and the Mosaic Law' in *Christianity Today* (16 March 1973). To bring out the alternative meaning let us look at two other translations. First, the New International Version:

> If men who are fighting hit a pregnant woman and she gives birth prematurely but there is no serious injury, the offender must be fined whatever the woman's husband demands and the court allows. But if there is serious injury, you are to take life for life, eye for eye, tooth for tooth . . .

Secondly, a rendering by Professor J. W. Fraser[12] of the Free Church of Scotland reads as follows:

> And when men struggle and they strike a pregnant woman, and her children come out, and there shall not be injury, he shall surely be fined as the woman's husband shall lay on him; and he shall give as the judges decide. But if there be an injury, thou shalt give life for life . . .

In their comments upon this portion of Scripture, Keil and Delitzsch maintain that:

1. The word 'fruit' (AV) should be 'child' (children). The Hebrew word yeled is translated variously in the Old Testament as 'child' (Gen. 21:16), 'young man' (Gen. 4:23), 'children' (Exod. 2:6), 'sons' (Ruth 1:5), 'young men' (2 Chron. 10:8), 'young ones' (Job 38:41).

2. In the Authorized Version the words 'depart from her' (Hebrew yāsā') can be translated 'come out of her' (as in Gen. 38:28,29, where the twins of Tamar 'came out'). In other words, the expression is used to describe the process of birth or delivery.

3. Since the clause 'and if any mischief follow' (v.23) does not specify to whom the mischief occurs, it must be understood to apply equally to mother or child—hence signifying that the law requires exactly the same penalty for injury to either.

Calvin deals with this passage in his *Harmony of the Pentateuch*, and regards it as an extension of the sixth commandment, 'Thou shalt not kill.' He writes:

> The passage at first sight is ambiguous, for if the word death [mischief] only applies to the pregnant woman, it would not have been a capital crime to put an end to the foetus, which would be a great absurdity; for the foetus, though enclosed in the womb of its mother, is already a human being, and it is almost a monstrous crime to rob it of the life which it has not yet begun to enjoy. If it seems more horrible to kill a man in his own house than in a field, because a man's home is his place of most secure refuge, it ought surely to be deemed more atrocious to destroy a foetus in the womb before it has come to light. On these grounds I am led to conclude, without hesitation, that the words 'if death [mischief] should follow' must be applied to the foetus as well as to the mother.

Similarly the Jewish scholar Cassuto puts forward a convincing argument that this is in fact the true meaning of the text.

The answer to the question of the status of the foetus, which is central to the whole debate, now becomes apparent. Although the Scriptures do not comment directly on the modern problem of therapeutic abortion, they do invest the foetus with a high status. In referring to it the Bible uses language perfectly consonant with normal 'human' experience. Obviously, inasmuch as the foetus is incapable of independent existence, it does not have the status of a completely independent human being, but in every other respect it is to be regarded as human.

Miscarriage

Those scriptures which speak of life in the womb tell us of the hand of God being active before birth. However, it might be argued that these texts serve little or no purpose and that the principles extracted from them cannot be applied in the matter of abortion. They say nothing, for example, concerning cases where a spontaneous miscarriage occurs.

However, the Bible *does* comment on such situations. In the poetical literature of Scripture we find three instances (Job 3:16, Ps. 58:8 and Eccles. 6:3), where an analogy is drawn between the life of a person and an aborted foetus, the product of a miscarriage. In the first instance, the life of Job himself is compared to an aborted foetus, while in the last two the comparison is drawn between an ungodly man and an aborted foetus. All three examples describe the miscarriage as an 'untimely birth' (Hebrew *nephel*).[13] How are the products of conception described? What is it that is miscarried? Job's answer is 'infants which never saw light'. The word which he uses for the products of conception (Hebrew *'ōlelîm*) occurs some 20 times in the Old Testament, and is always translated in the Authorized Version as 'infant(s)', 'child/children', 'babes', or once as 'little ones'. One of the most familiar of these verses is Psalm 8:2—'out of the mouth of babes (*'ōlelîm*) and sucklings hast thou ordained strength because of thine enemies'. Here then is an indication of the status given to a foetus. What is carried in the womb, and miscarried, is an infant or child.

Miscarriage and bereavement

There is a third source from which an understanding and appreciation of foetal status may be drawn. This is the Hebrew word translated 'miscarry', as in Hosea 9:14. There, speaking of the judgment of God which is to come upon Ephraim, Hosea pronounces this curse: 'Give them, O Lord: what wilt thou give? Give them a miscarrying womb and dry breasts.' Of interest and relevance to the present discussion is the fact that the Hebrew word for miscarry (*šākōl*) is sometimes used in the context of bereavement. Compare the following instances:

> And may God Almighty grant you mercy before the man so that he will let your other brother and Benjamin come back with you. As for me, if I am bereaved, I am bereaved.   Genesis 43:14

> I will take away sickness from among you, and none will miscarry or be barren in your land.   Exodus 23:25,26

It might be argued that if a man is bereaved of that which is human, then that which is miscarried is also human. If this is so, it gives another indication of the status of the foetus in Old Testament thought.

The soul

There are other problems raised in any consideration of the subject of abortion. Not least important of these is the question of the origin of the soul. One fertilized egg cell may divide into two, thus giving rise to two offspring. Is the soul introduced before or after division? Again, it is believed that in up to 50 per cent of all fertilized egg cells spontaneous miscarriage occurs. Do all of these have souls? An egg cell may be fertilized with a male cell and kept artificially in a fluid in a laboratory, a kind of 'test tube' foetus. This can be continued only to a certain stage of development. When the fertilized egg cell is discarded, is a soul also expelled?

The answer to all these questions is that we do not know. But biblical principles still hold, and these uncertainties should not diminish our concept of the importance of the foetus. The aim of the Christian is to preserve the lives of both mother and foetus wherever possible.

Sometimes the occasion arises where the mother's life is at stake—for example, when an expectant mother with severe heart disease places herself in danger should the pregnancy continue, and both mother and foetus might be involved in a high risk of death. In such a case (the writer believes) it would be the lesser of two evils to abort the foetus. The lower status of the foetus would justify this.

Other cases which cause much headache include those where pregnancy arises from rape, or where the foetus is known to have a severe physical or mental abnormality. In a case of genuine rape, it might be argued that the mental trauma to the mother would be so great that, should the pregnancy continue, there would be disastrous consequences in terms of mental suffering to the mother. In which case, the lesser of two evils would be to terminate the pregnancy. Similar arguments might apply where it is known that the mother-to-be is carrying a severely physically or mentally handicapped child. However, one cannot help but point out that most of the so-called therapeutic abortions which are taking place today are censured by the commandment 'Thou shalt not kill.'

THE CHRISTIAN'S ATTITUDE

Having formulated some biblical principles, the Christian is now able to face other problems, such as how to respond to the attitude generally displayed by society, and what are the practical consequences of abortion.

The Christian is entitled, and indeed required, to proclaim the law of God in a lawless society. In the experience of the writer many women, even though not committed Christians, are genuinely concerned to know what Christian teaching is in such matters. God's voice in Scripture is not to be silenced or subdued by us in the face of indifference or even antagonism. In the same way the Christian must speak out upon and safeguard the role of conscience with respect to the outworking of the Abortion Act. It is surely scandalous if people are penalized for no other reason than that their consciences are tender.

The practical consequences of abortion, of course, vary, and it should be emphasized that the Christian must give priority to biblical principles and not to pathological consequences. That there are such consequences is most certainly the case. From a review article by H. Gordon entitled 'Abortion as a method of population regulation: the problems', many points can be gleaned.[14] The reader may wish to refer to the review.

As far as psychiatric and emotional sequelae to termination of pregnancy are concerned, opinions and reports vary. One study reported on short-term psychiatric sequelae, and in its conclusions the following statement is made: 'Of 44 women interviewed six months after operation, the outcome was favourable for 30 patients (68%) and unfavourable for 14 patients (32%). The psychiatric status of 39 patients was improved or unchanged, and only 7 regretted the termination.'[15]

Whatever such results may be, the Christian must not base his arguments against abortion on the practical consequences. As treatment becomes more sophisticated, then presumably results will

132

change. The determining factors must be those found in the Word of God, and although on first appearance Scripture has little to say to the modern situation, it clearly establishes basic principles concerning the profoundly important status of the foetus.

2. Family Planning and Related Issues

It is now difficult to believe that a generation ago family planning was a taboo subject amongst Christians, and that indeed up until the beginning of this century it was almost universally accepted in the church that such practices were immoral. Now, of course, we live in a world where there are many pressures on the Christian to practise contraception. These include such factors as 'the population explosion', 'eugenic considerations', being emotionally 'ready' to have children and, of course, ensuring that the best facilities are available for their upbringing. Such has been the intrusion of 'the pill' into our everyday lives that we are now presented with the opposite danger—that of thoughtless contraception! However, the responsible, thinking Christian will not just accept the pressures of modern twentieth-century society as the controlling factor for his actions, but will wish to glean some understanding of biblical principles concerning such matters. The very title 'Family Planning' indicates that it is taken for granted that this discussion is applicable only to the 'family' or indeed only to husband and wife, and the matters are discussed within the setting of marriage.

Given these basic premises, to begin with we must ask an important question. Is there a final, authoritative teaching concerning such matters? The answer is clearly No: there is a spectrum of Protestant thought varying from the belief that *no* artificial methods of contraception are justified to the belief that *any* artificial method is justifiable.

As far as the Scripture is concerned there is no explicit teaching on these matters: on the other hand, there are certain implicit general principles which help us. Before we examine these principles it is important to point out that it is not our purpose to discuss the details of methods of contraception, except where there are more serious moral implications (an obvious example would be the use of so-called 'therapeutic abortion' as a family planning measure). Neither is this intended to be an exhaustive study; it is, rather, a stimulus to further thought and discussion.

GENERAL PRINCIPLES

When considering the Christian teaching of marriage we are thinking of a lifelong monogamous relationship between a man and a woman which is usually only terminated by the death of one of the partners. It represents the deepest possible relationship between two people. Although we can trace various themes running through Scripture illustrating various aspects of marriage, such as companionship, fulfilment, sexual pleasure and procreation, none of these facets can be taken in isolation from the others. The best description of marriage as a whole is that of the Bible: 'For this reason a man will leave his father and mother and be united to his wife, and the two will become one flesh' (Matt. 19:5). The description of marriage reaches its highest level in the New Testament when it is used as a figure to describe the relationship and love between Christ and His church: 'Husbands, love your wives, just as Christ loved the church' (Eph. 5:25).

In addition, it is important to note that in Scripture certain aspects of the marital relationship are discussed in isolation from others. For instance, in 1 Corinthians 7 sexual satisfaction is discussed *as an end in itself*, with no mention of procreation:

> The husband should fulfil his marital duty to his wife, and likewise the wife to her husband. The wife's body does not belong to her alone but also to her husband. In the same way, the husband's body does not belong to him alone but also to his wife. Do not deprive each other except by mutual consent and for a time, so that you may devote yourself to prayer. Then come together again so that Satan will not tempt you because of your lack of self-control.   1 Corinthians 7:3-5

Paul is obviously describing the marital relationship in terms of sexual pleasure, quite apart from any other aspect of marriage. We can go further then, and conclude that there is nothing in Scripture to suggest that all of the purposes of marriage must be present all of the time.

This principle can be enlarged, for despite differing emphases in the Old and New Testaments there is basic common ground. For example, the 'one flesh' principle runs through both. It is of interest to note that wherever this expression occurs in the Bible there is no mention of procreation as the object of sexual union. Indeed, fruitfulness is a blessing *added to* the 'one flesh'. What then are the purposes of marriage as seen in terms of this concept? One is for the completeness of man (Gen. 2:24; Matt. 19:5). Although the command to be fruitful and multiply is mentioned in

134

Genesis (1:28), there is no mention of procreation in Genesis 2:24; here the principle is rather that of marriage being ordained for the completeness of man. Genesis 2:18 prepares us for this: 'It is not good for the man to be alone. I will make a helper suitable for him.'

It was in this setting, then, that the 'one flesh' principle was ordained: its object was to provide for fellowship and companionship, and there is no reference to procreation. One writer has put it:

> God's plan provided for a companion who satisfied the unfulfilled yearning of man's heart. Woman was created for mutual fellowship and companionship. Man was to be a social creature and his wife was to be one with whom he might share love, trust, devotion and responsibility; she was to respond to his nature with understanding and love in reciprocal relationship. [16]

If this understanding of Scripture is right, we may note in passing that there is no justification for Roman Catholic opposition to family planning, based as it is on so-called 'natural law' theology. The following quotation from *Humanae Vitae* illustrates a kind of thinking which is inconsistent with the biblical teaching we have outlined: 'Nonetheless, the Church, calling men back to observance of the norms of natural law as interpreted by their constant doctrine, teaches that each and every married act (*quilibet matrimonii usus*) must remain open to the "transmission of life".' [17]

Passing mention must be made of Genesis 38:8-10, a passage which has been used by various writers to show biblical disapproval of contraception. However, the context seems to suggest that Onan practised 'coitus interruptus' in order to 'keep from producing offspring for his brother', and that God's punishment came on him for this reason. This is a more acceptable interpretation in the light of Leviticus 15:16-18, where the laws concerning 'uncleanness' are outlined. The point is that an emission of semen of itself is not regarded as a sinful act, since no sacrifice is demanded.

METHODS OF CONTRACEPTION

Having outlined the case for family planning in marriage, we proceed to ask the question, Are all methods of contraception open to the Christian? Here again difficulties arise, in that the Scripture has nothing directly to say on these matters and we have to argue from first principles. Having said this, it seems doubtful to us whether certain methods would be open to the Christian. For example, in view of what has been said about termination of pregnancy this cannot be advocated as an acceptable method of contraception, although it has been used very widely in many countries (e.g. Japan). Similarly, doubts arise concerning the use of intra-uterine devices such as the coil. We noted in the first part of this chapter that it is generally believed that the way in which these methods work is to prevent implantation of the fertilized ovum (egg cell). Some might therefore see this as a kind of 'therapeutic abortion'. Similarly the 'morning after' pill prevents implantation of the fertilized ovum, and is again a form of abortion. Other methods do not carry these ethical objections: they include mechanical barriers to fertilization (the sheath and cap), spermicidal creams and the contraceptive pill. Other very uncertain methods include restraint (with or without taking notice of the normal 'rhythm' for producing egg cells in the woman) and coitus interruptus. The problems in terms of stress and uncertainty in these latter methods make their use highly questionable.

Sterilization

Male or female sterilization is increasingly being advocated, usually as a contraceptive device. Whichever form is used, more or less permanent infertility is the result. There are a number of possible indications for sterilization, which have been conveniently categorized as eugenic, socio-economic, convenience, and prophylactic.[18]

Eugenic indications are considered where there is probability that offspring will be mentally or physically deformed, or both. This has been widely advocated in some Scandinavian countries. Socio-economic arguments are usually adopted in some underdeveloped countries, such as India, where the cheapest and most certain form of contraception is necessary. The use of sterilization (usually in developed countries) as an effective, certain way of family planning comes into the 'convenience' category. This includes most of the sterilizations carried out in Britain. Prophylactic indications exist where there would be serious health problems or a risk of death (to the woman), were further pregnancies to occur.

These indications are of course a simple way of categorizing the reasons used to justify sterilization. They do not deal with the question as to whether or not sterilization is ethical. As far as the Christian is concerned he will be concerned to know what the Bible says on this subject.

There were of course eunuchs in biblical times. These were men who had been castrated—usually by a subjugating race. However, the Jews were forbidden to do this. Not only so, but eunuchs were

136

excluded from communal religious worship (Deut. 23:1). Delitzsch comments: 'The reason for exclusion of emasculated persons from the congregation of the Lord . . . is to be found in the mutilation of the nature of man as created by God.'[19] We can certainly say that barrenness was frowned upon (and often regarded as a curse), and that infertility (male or female) produced by artificial sterilization was unacceptable before God.

Surely, therefore, the Christian should at least adopt a 'conservative view' towards sterilization, particularly since other methods of contraception are available. It is the writer's personal belief that sterilization of husband or wife should only be considered where there would be serious risk to the health or life of the woman if she should become pregnant, or where contraception is impractical on health grounds.

The above represents an outline of basic Protestant thinking on the matter of family planning. It is hoped that it will provide a basis for further discussion on these matters. In conclusion it must be underlined that it is *family planning* which has been discussed, and not simply contraception. This is an important point because it reminds us that 'fruitfulness' is still described by the Scriptures as a blessing of God. In Genesis 1:28 we read, 'God blessed them [the man and the woman] and said to them, "Be fruitful and increase in number; fill the earth and subdue it."' In the light of this, except in cases where to have children would constitute a serious health risk to the wife, it is difficult to see how a Christian couple can justify denying themselves, through lifelong contraception, this blessing which they are commanded to receive from God.

APPENDIX

Most terminations of pregnancy are carried out under the so-called 'socio-economic' conditions of the Act. The relevant part of the Act is quoted in full as follows:

1. Subject to the provisions of this section, a person shall not be guilty of an offence under the law relating to abortion when a pregnancy is terminated by a registered medical practitioner if two registered medical practitioners are of the opinion, formed in good faith:

   a) that the continuance of the pregnancy would involve risk to the life of the pregnant woman, or of **injury** to the physical or **mental health of the pregnant woman or any existing children of her family**, greater than if the pregnancy were terminated; or

   b) that there is a substantial risk that if the child were born it would suffer from such physical or mental abnormalities as to be seriously handicapped.

2. In determining whether the continuance of a pregnancy would involve such risk of injury to health as is mentioned in paragraph (a) of subsection (1) of this section, **account may be taken of the pregnant woman's actual or reasonably foreseeable environment.**

The qualification, 'injury to the mental health of the pregnant woman or any existing children of her family' is sometimes extended to mean even the mildest feelings of inconvenience which the individual experiences. It is the writer's opinion that the Christian must oppose this absolutely (in contrast to the genuine case where the mother might suffer an attack of insanity).

NOTES

1 Arnold Gillespie, 'Techniques of Abortion', *British Journal of Hospital Medicine*, 9:3 (1973), pp.309-16.

2 R. F. R. Gardner, an article in the *International Reformed Bulletin* (1972).

3 *Abortion Act* (HMSO, 1967). See Appendix for further details of the legal grounds for abortion.

4 Harley S. Smyth, *Biblical Allusions to Life before Birth* (Christian Medical Fellowship, 1975).

5 R. F. R. Gardner, *Abortion: the Personal Dilemma* (Paternoster Press, 1972).

6 Francis Schaeffer, 'No Compromise', *Christian Graduate*, 28:2 (1975), p.33.

7 A. Gillespie, 'Techniques of Abortion'.

8 Abbott-Smith, *A Manual Greek Lexicon of the New Testament* (T. & T. Clark, 1964).

9 John Calvin, *Harmony of the Pentateuch* (Calvin Translation Society, 1854), vol. 3, pp.41-2.

10 Keil and Delitzsch, *A Biblical Commentary on the Old Testament* (Eerdmans, 1971), The Pentateuch, vol. 2, pp.134-5.

11 U. Cassuto, *A Commentary on the Book of Exodus* (Magues Press, Hebrew University, 1967), pp.272-8.

12 J.W. Fraser, in a personal letter to the author.

13 *The Englishman's Hebrew and Chaldee Concordance* (Bagster, 1963).

14 H. Gordon, 'Abortion as a method of population regulation: the problems', *British Journal of Hospital Medicine*, 9:3 (1973), pp.303-6.

15 B. Lask, 'Short-term Psychiatric Sequelae to Therapeutic Termination of Pregnancy', *British Journal of Psychiatry*, 126 (February 1975), pp.173-7.

16 'Birth Control and the Christian', *A Protestant Symposium on the Control of Human Reproduction* (Tyndale House, Wheaton, Illinois, 1969).

17 *Humanae Vitae* (July 1968)—a Papal Encyclical.

18 S. Scorer and A. Wing, *Decision Making in Medicine* (Edward Arnold, 1979).

19 Keil and Delitzsch, *Commentary* (Eerdmans, 1971), The Pentateuch, vol. 3.

FURTHER READING

There is a considerable amount of literature on abortion, although much of it is written without direct reference to family life. A number of books and articles are mentioned in the notes. A standard book is Gardner's *Abortion: The Personal Dilemma* (Paternoster Press, 1972). More recent discussions can be found in C. G. Scorer, *Life in Our Hands* (Inter-Varsity Press, 1978), N. Anderson, *Issues of Life and Death* (Hodder & Stoughton, 1976), and F. A. Schaeffer and C. E. Koop, *Whatever Happened to the Human Race?* (Marshalls, 1980). A helpful short discussion of the subject has been written by Peter Barnes, *Open Your Mouth for the Dumb* (Banner of Truth, 1984).

With respect to family planning, in addition to the references given in the chapter notes, the books by Anderson and (more fully) Scorer discuss the topic further.

Bibliography

A. BOOKS

J. E. Adams, *Christian Living in the Home* (Baker, 1972).

J. E. Adams, *Marriage, Divorce and Remarriage in the Bible* (Presbyterian & Reformed, 1980).

J. E. Adams, *Update on Christian Counselling II* (Presbyterian & Reformed, 1981).

A. Alexander, *Thoughts on Religious Experience* (Banner of Truth, 1967).

A. Anderson, *Marriage, Divorce and Remarriage* (Fellowship of Independent Evangelical Churches, 1980).

N. Anderson, *Issues of Life and Death* (Hodder & Stoughton, 1976).

Annual Abstract of Statistics, published annually for the Central Statistical Office by HMSO.

P. Barnes, *Open Your Mouth For the Dumb* (Banner of Truth, 1984).

H. M. Carson, *Facing Suffering* (Evangelical Press, 1978).

L. Christenson, *The Christian Family* (Bethany Fellowship, 1970).

M. E. Clark, *Choosing Your Career* (Presbyterian & Reformed, 1981).

J. Dobson, *Preparing For Adolescence* (Vision House, 1978).

J. Dobson, *Hide or Seek?* (Hodder & Stoughton, 1982).

J. Eareckson, *Joni* (Pickering & Inglis, 1978).

J. Eareckson and S. Estes, *A Step Further* (Pickering & Inglis, 1979).

Families in the Future (Study Commission on the Family, 1983).

D. Field, *Taking Sides* (Inter-Varsity Press, 1975).

S. T. Foh, *Women and the Word of God* (Presbyterian & Reformed, 1979).

R. F. R. Gardner, *Abortion: The Personal Dilemma* (Paternoster Press, 1972).

C. Gilhuis, *Conversations on Growing Older* (Eerdmans, 1977).

E. M. B. Green, *Evangelism in the Early Church* (Hodder & Stoughton, 1970).

Happy Families? (Study Commission on the Family, 1980).

R. Holman, *Poverty: Explanations of Social Deprivation* (Martin Robertson, 1978).

J. Hurley, *Man and Woman in Biblical Perspective* (Inter-Varsity Press, 1981).

Illustrated Bible Dictionary (Inter-Varsity Press, 1980).

P. Jeffery, *Our Present Sufferings* (Evangelical Press of Wales, 1982).

O. R. Johnston, *Who Needs the Family?* (Hodder & Stoughton, 1979).

D. P. Kingdon, *Children of Abraham* (Carey Press, 1973).

D. M. Lloyd-Jones, *Studies in the Sermon on the Mount* (Inter-Varsity Fellowship, 1959).

D. M. Lloyd-Jones, *Faith on Trial* (Inter-Varsity Press, 1965).

D. M. Lloyd-Jones, *Life in the Spirit* (Banner of Truth, 1974).

W. Mack, *How to Develop Deep Unity in the Marriage Relationship* (Presbyterian & Reformed, 1977).

S. Macaulay, *Something Beautiful from God* (Marshall, Morgan & Scott, 1980).

J. Murray, *Principles of Conduct* (Inter-Varsity Press, 1957).

J. Murray, *Divorce* (Presbyterian & Reformed, 1961).

New Bible Dictionary (Inter-Varsity Press, 1962).

J. Newton, *Letters* (Banner of Truth, 1960).

J. Owen, 'The Glory of Christ', *Works* (Banner of Truth, 1965), vol. 1, pp.432-61.

J. I. Packer, *Knowing God* (Hodder & Stoughton, 1975).

D. C. Potter, *Too Soon to Die* (Evangelical Press, 1982).

M. Radius, *Ninety Story Sermons For Children's Church* (Baker, 1966).

M. Radius, *Two Spies on a Rooftop* (Baker, 1968).

B. Ray, *Withhold Not Correction* (Baker, 1970).

S. Rees (ed.) *The Role of Women* (Inter-Varsity Press, 1984).

J. O. Sanders, *Enjoying Growing Old* (Kingsway, 1981).

F. A. Schaeffer and C. E. Koop, *Whatever Happened to the Human Race?* (Marshalls, 1980).

M. Schoolland, *Leading Little Ones to God* (Banner of Truth, 1970).

C. G. Scorer, *Life in Our Hands* (Inter-Varsity Press, 1978).

Social Trends, HMSO, published annually for Central Statistical Office.

A. M. Stibbs, *Family Life Today* (Marcham Manor Press, n.d.).

A. Storkey, *A Christian Social Perspective* (Inter-Varsity Press, 1979).

J. Stott, *Divorce* (Falcon, 1971).

J. Stott, *Issues Facing Christians Today* (Marshall, Morgan & Scott, 1984).

Values and the Changing Family (Study Commission on the Family, 1980).

J. White, *Parents in Pain* (Inter-Varsity Press, 1980).

B. ARTICLES

G. and C. Bahnsen, 'Adoption: Theological Treasure and Model for the Home', *Journal of Christian Reconstruction*, 4 (1977-8), pp.130-48.

H. M. Carson, 'Divorce', *Banner of Truth*, 209 (February 1981), pp.20-6.

P. Henry, 'The Duties of the Aged', *Banner of Truth*, 67 (April 1969), pp.30-3.

H. R. Jones, 'Should a Christian Marry a Non-Christian, and Should the Ceremony Take Place in an Evangelical Church?', *Foundations*, 9 (1982), pp.16-25.

J. Marsh, 'On the Subject of Growing Old', *Christian Graduate*, 31 (December 1978), pp.8-10.

G. North, 'Family Authority and Protestant Sacerdotalism', *Journal of Christian Reconstruction*, 4 (1977-8), pp.87-129.

C. AUDIO TAPES

J. E. Adams, *The Christian Family* (Ambassador Productions Ltd., 1980). 5 Tapes.

A. N. Martin, *Distinctive Sexual Identity* (Trinity Pulpit). 4 Tapes

D. C. Potter, *Communicating the Gospel to Handicapped People* (Association of Christian Teachers).

Suffering (Communications, 12 Abbey Close, Abingdon, Oxon OX14 3JD).

G. Thomas, *Biblical Perspectives on the Family* (Christian Reformed Tapes). 20 Tapes

Most of these cassettes can be obtained from Christian Reformed Tapes, 72 High Street, Inverurie, Aberdeenshire, AB5 9XS. The Association of Christian Teachers is at Stapleford House, Wesley Place, Stapleford, Nottingham, NG9 8PD.

Index of Scripture References

General Index

Gardner, R. F. R. 138n., 139
Gilhuis, Cornelis 105
Gillespie, A. 127, 138n.
Gordon, H. 132, 139n.
Gore, Charles 111f.
Grandparents 73f.
Green, E. M. B. 69n.

Handicapped children 11, 19, 71-9
  conversion of 78, 79
  mental handicap 72, 79
  trends 14
Hendriksen, William 102, 120n.
Henry, Matthew 26, 43, 59, 97
Henry, Philip 105
Hodge, Charles 51
Holman, Robert 13, 15n.
Hospitality 25f.
Hurley, James 26n., 27
Husbands 10, 19, 23f., 32f., 37-44

Illegitimacy 13, 29
Image of God 18f., 34f., 36, 75

Jeffery, Peter 79
Judaism 20

Keil and Delitzsch, 128, 129, 139n.
Kline, Meredith 27n.
Koop, C. E. 139

Lask, B. 139n.
Leach, Edmund 10
Lloyd-Jones, D. M. 27, 47, 79,
  104, 120n.

Macaulay, Susan 79
McCrae, Kenneth 100
Mack, Wayne 47, 60
Marriage
  and creation 30
  and God's relation to the
    church 20f., 37f.
  apostolic teaching on 29-46
  arranged marriages 18
  attitudes to 10
  remarriage 12f., 111, 112f., 116
  unbelieving partners 23f., 26n.,
    27n., 113-16, 117f.
Marsh, John 105

Martin, A. N. 28, 51
Martyn, Henry 22
Muggeridge, Malcolm 124
Murray, John 27n., 47, 109, 111,
  112, 120n.

Owen, John 105

Packer, J. I. 79
Parenthood 49-60, 82-7, 89-91
  attitudes to 10
  authority of 10, 11, 51-9, 62,
    67f.
  discipline 53-5, 83f.
  instruction of children 56-9,
    61f.
  Prayer 21, 46, 51, 58f.
  Providence 12

Radius, Marianne 60
Rees, Shirley 28
Roman Catholic Church 9, 20, 83,
  135

Sanctification 9, 23
Sanders, Oswald 100, 105
Schaeffer, Francis 124, 126f.,
  138n., 139
Schoolland, Marian 58, 60
Scorer, C. G. 139
Scripture
  authority of 11, 26n., 113
  contemporary application 12,
    18
  relation of Old and New
    Testaments 17f., 21-3
Shakespeare, William 93
Singleness 22f.
Single parents 13, 14, 24, 69n.
Smyth, Harley 126, 138n.
Social Welfare Agencies 75, 82-4,
  85f., 88f., 103, 104
Spock, Benjamin 53
Spurgeon, Charles H. 91f.
Sterilization 11, 14, 136f.
Stibbs, Alan 61, 69n.
Storkey, Alan 10, 15n.
Stott, John 113, 116f., 120n., 124
Suffering 72-4
Sunday schools 56, 58f.

147

Taylor, Thomas 99, 100
Teenagers 55f., 66-9
Thomas, Geoffrey 27

Wesley, Charles 95
White, John 60, 70
Whitefield, George 91f.

Wives 23f.
  submission 24, 32-8
  'weaker vessel' 24, 36f.
Women's movement 18, 19, 29, 37
World 9
Worship 9, 58f.